DAVID & CHARLES SOURCES FOR SOCIAL & ECONOMIC HISTORY

The Factory System

VOLUME I: BIRTH AND GROWTH

FREE TRADE
Norman McCord
Reader in Modern History
University of Newcastle upon Tyne

in preparation

THE FACTORY SYSTEM   VOLUME II THE FACTORY SYSTEM AND
SOCIETY
J. T. Ward
Senior Lecturer in Economic History
University of Strathclyde

POOR LAW
Michael E. Rose
Lecturer in History, University of Manchester

READINGS IN THE DEVELOPMENT OF ECONOMIC ANALYSIS
R. D. C. Black
Professor of Economics, The Queen's University of Belfast

DAVID & CHARLES SOURCES FOR SOCIAL & ECONOMIC HISTORY

J. T. WARD
Senior Lecturer in Economic History
University of Strathclyde

The Factory System

System

VOLUME I: BIRTH AND GROWTH

DAVID & CHARLES : NEWTON ABBOT

7153 4901 5

Set in Baskerville 11 pt 2 pt leaded
and printed in Great Britain
by Latimer Trend & Company Limited Plymouth
for David & Charles (Publishers) Limited
South Devon House   Newton Abbot   Devon

Contents

PART THREE: THE FACTORY SYSTEM ESTABLISHED

Introduction

'Whirr! whirr! all by wheels!—whiz! whiz! all by steam! The armies of the English ride upon the vapours of boiling cauldrons, and their horses are flaming coals!—whirr! whirr! all by wheels!—whiz! whiz! all by steam!' Such was the picture of England in 1834 sketched for the traveller A. W. Kinglake by an Ottoman pasha. As a dramatic description of a new and unique system it was not without merit; and as a Turkish official's view of industrial Britain it had some significance. But British writers have always been divided in their attitudes to the great industrial changes of the late eighteenth and early nineteenth centuries; and even contemporary observers did not unanimously share the pasha's delight in whirring and whizzing machines.

The classic Industrial Revolution—the first, pioneering series of industrial, commercial and technological innovations—had many results. It led transport into the age of steam locomotives, called into being much of the engineering industry, largely transferred ancient textile trades from the worker's home to the factory and mill, vastly extended the metallurgical industries, provoked extensive colliery development, inaugurated change in virtually every institution, set off a train of immense social changes and fundamentally altered both the landscape and many people's lives. And it had many causes; numerous features of a particular stage of British history encouraged and sustained industrial development.

The *laisser-faire* doctrines announced in the eighteenth cen-

tury and confidently asserted in the nineteenth had little influence during the period of industrial 'take-off'; most of the
apparatus of old-style State interference remained in being
until the early decades of the nineteenth century. But even a
mercantilist Britain was comparatively free, politically, economi-
cally and regionally, and was unfettered by the absolutist,
feudal or social sanctions widely enforced in Europe. This freedom from government control was partly accidental—no
thoroughgoing system of bureaucratic interference could be
expected in a society where local administration was dominated
by countless Squire Westerns—but it was important in that it
left enterprise almost uniquely free.

Various factors contributed to the make-up of the type of
society in which this enterprise could flourish. The long improvement of British agriculture led to increased rents, and some of
the increase was used, directly or indirectly, by enlightened
landowners to finance industrial ventures. Low interest rates on
government loans, particularly after the creation of 3 per cent
Consols in 1757, eased the capitalisation of industry, despite
legal restraints on company promotion. And a banking net-
work, however imperfectly, channelled capital to industry and
speeded commercial processes by providing notes, transferring
bills of exchange, and settling accounts. Meanwhile, the landowners had presided over and largely financed major transport
improvements, through turnpike trusts and canal and river
undertakings. And many sons of the urban middle classes were
preparing themselves for industrial or commercial careers at
new schools (not all of them 'dissenting academies') with wider
curricula than the classical diet of the old public and grammar
schools. Eighteenth-century society was thus changing, sometimes ahead of and sometimes simultaneously with the process
of industrial change. The infrastructure which permitted an
industrial revolution to occur was gradually evolving, but was far
from being complete when the new technology started to develop.

Demography was at least as important as economics and
technology. Whether through a rising birth-rate or a falling

death-rate (or both), to the consternation of the Rev Thomas
Malthus late eighteenth-century Britain experienced something
of a population explosion. Both the causes and the chronology of
this population growth are debated by historians; but the ulti-
mate importance of the 'demographic revolution' to economic
expansion is obvious. In the long run, an increased population
would raise an already increasing demand for goods. But
traditional industrial organisation was not geared to meet such
raised demand levels. The textile merchant, for instance, in
order to expand his trade must put out material to distant
home-workers, with inevitable results, especially in times of
boom: the spinning of Norwich wool in Westmorland probably
encouraged the stealing of material and certainly, because of
transport costs, increased the price of yarn.

Rising demand at home and abroad, caused by increased
affluence in the higher echelons of society and increased numbers among all orders, must have led early industrialists to
view with concern any increase in cost. Consequently employers
would welcome any technological improvement likely to raise
productivity and reduce expense; the Manchester men who
first interested Dr Cartwright in the power-loom were typical.
A succession of inventors from all ranks of the social hierarchy,
from impoverished working-men to enthusiastic aristocrats,
sought to provide the new machines and techniques which
would revolutionise each industry. The spate of inventions—to
some extent reflected in the rising number of patents granted—
undoubtedly owed much to particularly talented or venturesome individuals. But it also depended upon longer-term considerations: much of British society tended to admire the inventor, at a time when 'feudal' and other influences restrained
his Continental colleague. The Royal Society of 1660, the
Society of Arts of 1754, Glasgow University, Parliamentary
grants to meritorious inventors, and assorted local groups
(especially the celebrated Lunar Society in Birmingham) made
varying contributions to the technological revolution; and their
activities demonstrated social attitudes.

A growing population, even rudimentary banking services, a notable group of inventors, improved transport facilities, and variably sustained previous growth in some industrial areas were all important; and so were the facts that Britain was a 'free trade area', an imperial power, and internally peaceful. The possession of these 'virtues' was unique in the mid-eighteenth century, though other nations had more capital, people, and land area. But social factors provided an additional impetus to British growth beyond those stimuli given by economic, technological, political and geographic facts. To Dr Johnson it seemed that 'the age was running mad after innovation'. And within a century Thomas Carlyle was protesting that 'England was full of wealth, of multifarious produce, supply for human want in every kind; yet England was dying of inanition'. The voice of protest slowly, almost imperceptibly, changed from being anti-industrialist to anti-capitalist: outright opponents of industrialisation later became rare, but there was for long a middle period when the target of protest was not precisely defined. On the whole, however, British society, social structure, and social attitudes in the eighteenth century provided an environment receptive to change.

The small British aristocracy—titled and untitled landowners in the main—differed from the large European classes of nobles. Primogeniture perpetuated what radicals were later to condemn as a 'land monopoly'; but it also forced younger sons of the landed classes into the world of business, trade, religion, the professions, and military service. British noblemen were never turned into the gilded moths flitting about Versailles or the boorish warlords strutting around Potsdam. They would sensibly seek to augment rural rent-rolls by industrial, urban, mineral and other non-agricultural interests, rarely fearing any loss of caste status; and a few of them became considerable industrialists. At the other end of the social scale, the rural labourer—ill-paid, illiterate, badly housed and constantly taught the virtues of subservient deference to his 'betters'— might be subject to the tyranny of hirings, of enforced 'custom',

of harsh summary 'justice', and of perpetual personal subjuga-
tion. But he was legally a free man, not a permanent serf; and,
while contracts, poverty, ignorance, personal inclination, family
obligations, or squirearchic control might hinder his mobility,
he was legally free to move. Many agricultural families did
move to the industrial centres, driven by both the attraction of
new work and their loss of status in the increasingly enclosed
countryside.

For Britain's major group of industries, the textile trades old
and new, the Industrial Revolution brought immense changes
in established tradition. The new machinery was more easily
adopted in the expanding cotton industry than in the old woollen
and worsted districts. The growing sophistication and expense
of the machines and constant hopes of reducing costs led to the
rapid expansion of the factory system. And the need for water
power restricted the choice of sites for the early spinning mills:
the fast rivers and streams of the Pennines, parts of the Midlands and some districts of Scotland had obvious attractions.
The supply of labour in some such areas might prove trouble-
some, though local scarcity could be countered by the importation of pauper or orphan children and both the climate and
landscape of North-Western England and Western Scotland
proved particularly desirable for cotton manufacture. When
steam power became dominant and mills and factories could
more generally be sited in the towns, employers usually moved
only a short distance, often to the nearest sizeable community.

The entrepreneurs who ordered these changes were the great
decision-makers of the Industrial Revolution. Historians have
noted that many prominent members of this new and growing
middle class were religious nonconformists. Various reasons for
this fact have been propounded. Opponents of Protestantism
and capitalism have been tempted to date both 'heresies'
from the Reformation. But the English Reformation was less
revolutionary than those of Europe, and the Church remained
Catholic: Protestantism only started to have importance with
the rise of the seventeenth-century sects. The concomitant of a

theological individualism which dispensed with the inter-
mediary services of the priest might be an economic individualism; and certainly the Puritan virtues of hard work, thrift, and
personal moderation fitted very well with the capitalist ethic
and the requirements of early entrepreneurship, particularly
when Puritan condemnations of greed and self-indulgent
wealth were forgotten. Furthermore, eighteenth-century nonconformists were legally debarred (though in practice not entirely prohibited) from several professions and posts, while
commerce and industry remained open to them. And dissenting
attitudes to children, both at school and in the home, may have
influenced some embryonic businessmen. While it is important
to remember that the pioneer business organisers included
Tories as well as Liberals and Anglican Churchmen as well as
Protestant dissenters, the extension of entrepreneurial and Industrial Revolution studies has shown that the historian must
always take account of the work of other social scientists interested in the phenomena of *laisser-faire* capitalism and liberal
capitalists. Not only the economist and the politician, but also
the geographer, the sociologist, the administrator, and the
psychologist, can make contributions to the continuing debate
over the causes, nature, and consequences of the Industrial
Revolution. Certainly, the 'easiest' of traditional explanations
have been marred by the failure of twentieth-century under-
developed nations with large populations, large amounts of
cheap or free capital, and generous donations of technical
equipment and expertise, to take off into any sustained growth
apart from that of population. A completely satisfying explana-
tion of the dynamic of the Industrial Revolution is elusive; and
consequently it is worth seeking.

The following extracts deal with the experience of the textile
industries during the classic stages of the British Industrial
Revolution. The views of contemporary observers and of early
historians are not, of course, definitive; but they do provide
some of the essential tools of the historian. In the selection of
material, an attempt has been made to balance the extracts in

order to give a picture of different industries, different stages of development, different regions and different attitudes. Both celebrated and neglected accounts are quoted, but nothing from either type of publication has been included for any purely melodramatic effect. This book is offered to the reader not as an attempt to provide answers to a long-continued series of discussions and controversies, but in the hope that an assorted collection of views and accounts may increase the student's involvement in the debate.

J. T. WARD
The University of Strathclyde

PART ONE

Before the Factory System

'The making of cloth within all parts of the realm is the greatest occupation and living of the poor commons of this land,' Parliament announced in 1454. For centuries the woollen industry retained its dominant position, with a great variety of local specialities. Protected by Government and admired by generations of tourists, it long remained England's major exporting industry. From the late middle ages the fulling mills magnetised the industry towards the banks of quickly moving rivers, capable of moving wheels which drove the hammers to felt the cloth. Woollen and worsted manufacture still enjoyed a prestigious status in the eighteenth century: the merchants dominated the town oligarchies and regularly marked business success by entering the landed gentry; the various stages of the domestic system still involved large numbers of virtually independent small weavers (particularly in Yorkshire); and yarn was spun almost throughout the country. But other textile industries, often themselves well established, were also developing, and a vast new range of technological changes and financial and managerial techniques was being evolved. The following sections describe various aspects of the textile industries on the eve of the Industrial Revolution.

The Norwich Worsted Industry   From the late middle ages England's national industry was divided between woollen and worsted sections. Worsted production was gradually concentrated in East Anglia, where the great 'wool churches' still bear witness to the wealth of the medieval merchants, and Norwich became an important industrial centre. The worsted masters 'put out' wool over a wide area and gave the ancient city a long prosperity. But from about 1770 Norfolk production was overtaken by that of the West Riding, which more easily adopted the new technology. Arthur Young (1741–1820) failed as a local farmer, but was a perceptive agricultural journalist who became secretary of the newly created Board of Agriculture in 1793. In 1771 he described the industry of the county town.

1   The city of *Norwich* is one of the most considerable in *England* after *London* . . .

The staple manufactures are crapes and camblets; besides which they make in great abundance damasks, sattins, alopeens, &c., &c., &c. They work up the *Leicestershire* and *Lincolnshire* wool chiefly, which is brought here for combing and spinning, while the *Norfolk* wool goes to Yorkshire for carding and cloths . . .

The earnings of the manufacturers are various, but in general high.

Men on an average do not exceed 5*s.* a week; but then many women earn as much: and boys of 15 or 16 likewise the same . . .

The weaving man and his boy, who now earn in general 7*s.* a week, could earn with ease 11*s.* if industrious.—But it is remarkable, that those men and their families who earn but 6*s.* a week, are much happier and better off than those who earn 2*s.* or 3*s.* extraordinary; for such extra earnings are mostly spent at the alehouse, or in idleness, which prejudice their following work. This is precisely the same effect as they have found when the prices of provisions have been very cheap; it results from the same cause. And this city has been very often pestered with mobs and insurrections under the pretence of an high price of provisions, merely because such dearness would not allow the men that portion of idleness and other indulgence which low rates throw them into.

. . . In respect to the present state of the manufacture, it is neither brisk, nor very dull. They could execute more orders

B

than they have; and some among them complain because they have not so great a trade as during the war; for then they could not answer the demand, for it was so uncommonly great (from 1743 to 1763 was their famous aera). This was however owing in some measure to many manufacturers exporting so largely on speculation, that the markets have been overstocked ever since;—and have occasioned that falling off which has been perceived since.—Indeed the unfortunate difference subsisting between *Great Britain* and the colonies is a great injury to them. Arthur Young. *The Farmer's Tour through the East of England*, 4 vols, 1771, II, 74–7

Sir Frederick Morton Eden (1766–1809), 2nd baronet of Truir, spent much of his energy on investigating the conditions of the eighteenth-century poor. His classic three-volume work is a vital source on the operation of the Poor Law and on many other aspects of eighteenth-century life. A member of an old Durham dynasty, Eden broke new ground by putting his practical knowledge to good use as founder and chairman of the Globe Insurance Company. He visited Norwich during a period of growing difficulty, when the war against revolutionary France and increasing Northern competition were bringing the city's golden age to an end.

2   The City of Norwich, comprehending 32 parishes, and 3 or 4 hamlets, and containing, in extent, about 8 square miles, is incorporated for the maintenance of it's Poor. It's population was ascertained in 1693, when it was found to amount to 28,881 souls; and again in 1752, when it was found to have increased to 36,169: it's present population is estimated at 40,000 inhabitants; but that number appears, from the subjoined tables of baptisms and burials, to be rather exaggerated.

The number of houses, etc. assessed to the window-tax is 2200: the number exempted could not be ascertained, but must be more considerable.

There are 370 ale-houses in Norwich.

The land-tax produces £8518. 11s. 11d. The rent of land, in some places near Norwich, is £5 an acre; but farms in general, in the vicinity of the city, let at about £1 an acre.

A cotton manufactory was established here about 7 years ago; but the staple manufactures of Norwich are camblets, and other worsted stuffs, of various denominations. It is probable, that more hands without the city, than within it, are employed in the manufactures; for, in 1771, Arthur Young calculated the number of looms in and near Norwich, at 12,000; and, allowing 6 persons to a loom, reckoned the number of people employed in this manufacture to be 72,000, and the amount of the stuffs sent annually from Norwich to exceed a million sterling.*

The Norwich trade has for some years been in a declining state, which is ascribed to the following causes: to the prevalent taste for wearing cottons, which has necessarily lessened the consumption of stuffs†; the low wages of the weavers and spinners, who are, in a considerable degree at the mercy of the manufacturers, and are not supposed to receive better pay than

---

* Eastern Tour, ii. 79.

† The Woollen manufacture, considering all its branches, is, no doubt, a more important national concern than the cotton manufacture. It would seem, however, that the cottons of Manchester create more employment than the Norwich stuffs. The general languor of the woollen business seems to have been principally owing to the difficulty of introducing machinery; the improvements of which have given cottons a decided advantage. The author of a pamphlet, written in 1788, asserts, that, not above twenty years before his time, the whole cotton trade of Great Britain did not return £2,000,001 to the country, for the raw materials, combined with the labour of the people; and at that period, before the introduction of the water-machinery, and hand-engines, the power of the single wheel could not exceed 50,000 spindles, employed in spinning the cotton-wool into yarn; but, at that moment, the power of spindles thus employed, amounted to two millions; and the gross return for the raw materials and labour, exceeded seven millions sterling. It was about the year 1784, that the expiration of Sir Richard Arkwright's patent caused the erection of water-machines for the spinning of warps, in all parts of the country; with which the hand-engines, for the spinning of weft, kept proportion. At the time he wrote, he estimated the number of

they did 20 years ago; and, lastly, to the war, which has put a
stop to the exportation of stuffs to France, Flanders, and
Holland, and, from the high price of insurance, much reduced
the trade to other countries. The merchants and manufacturers
are now overstocked with goods; and the weavers are, consequently, very ill supplied with work, and, what is worse, are
obliged to work up the worst materials. While business was
brisk, an industrious weaver might earn £1. 1s. a week, from
fine work; and from coarser work, 12s. a week. The average
earnings of weavers, at present, are thought not to exceed 7s. or
8s. a week. Women weavers earn from 5s. to 6s. a week.
Females, however, are principally employed in spinning, reel-
ing, winding, etc., in which they earn from 2s. to 4s. a week. Of
late, the wages, both of women and children, have been very
low; but business, since the beginning of this month, has been
rather brisk, from a notion that peace is not very distant.

The prices of provisions, at present, are: beef, 5½d. the pound;
mutton, from 5d. to 6d.; veal, from 4d. to 5d.; pork, from 7d.
to 8d.; bacon, 10d.; milk, ¾d. the pint; eggs, two for 1d.   Sir
Frederick Morton Eden. *The State of the Poor: or, An History of
the Labouring Classes in England, from the Conquest to the Present
Period*, 1797, II, 477–9

Water-mills, or machines, at   —   —   —   —   —   143
Mule-jennies, or machines, consisting of 90 spindles each   —   550
Hand-jennies, of 80 spindles each   —   —   —   —   20,070
Of the water-mills, 123 are in England, and 19 in Scotland.
    Of those in England,

Lancashire has 41	Cheshire has 8
Derbyshire 22	Staffordshire 7
Nottinghamshire 17	Westmorland 5
Yorkshire 11	Flintshire 3

These establishments, when in full work, are estimated to give employment
to about 26,000 men, 31,000 women, and 53,000 children, in spinning
alone; and, in all the subsequent stages of the manufacture, the number of
the persons employed, is estimated at 133,000 men, 59,000 women, and
48,000 children; making an aggregate of 159,000 men, 90,000 women, and
101,000 children; in all, 350,000 persons employed in the cotton manufacture . . .

The Yorkshire Woollen Industry   Yorkshire, and particularly the West Riding, was for centuries a major woollen
area. Under the early 'domestic system' it generally produced
coarse cloths, but by the early eighteenth century Yorkshire
industry was becoming more sophisticated in both organisation
and product. Riverside activity developed around the homes of
small manufacturers and fullers, while cloth markets in the
principal towns became thriving mercantile centres. Daniel
Defoe (1659?–1731), journalist, novelist, party pamphleteer,
unsuccessful merchant, and secret agent, published a celebrated
account of the woollen area in 1726; it was probably based on
observations recorded in the early eighteenth century.

---

3 But now I must observe to you, that after having pass'd the
second hill and come down into the valley again, and so still the
nearer we came to Hallifax, we found the houses thicker, and
the villages greater in every bottom; and not only so, but the
sides of the hills, which were very steep every way, were spread
with houses, and that very thick; for the land being divided into
small enclosures, that is to say, from two acres to six or seven
acres each, seldom more; every three or four pieces of land
had a house belonging to it.

  Then it was I began to perceive the reason and nature of the
thing, and found that this division of the land into small pieces,
and scattering of the dwellings, was occasioned by, and done
for the convenience of the business which the people were
generally employ'd in, and that, as I said before, though we
saw no people stirring without doors, yet they were all full
within; for, in short, this whole country, however mountainous,
and that no sooner we were down one hill but we mounted
another, is yet infinitely full of people; those people all full of
business; not a beggar, not an idle person to be seen, except
here and there an alms-house, where people antient, decrepid,
and past labour, might perhaps be found; for it is observable,
that the people here, however laborious, generally live to a

great age, a certain testimony to the goodness and wholesom-
ness of the country, which is, without doubt, as healthy as any
part of England; nor is the health of the people lessen'd, but
help'd and establish'd by their being constantly employ'd, and,
as we call it, their working hard; so that they find a double
advantage by their being always in business.

This business is the clothing trade, for the convenience of
which the houses are thus scattered and spread upon the sides
of the hills, as above, even from the bottom to the top; the
reason is this; such has been the bounty of nature to this otherwise frightful country, that two things essential to the business,
as well as to the ease of the people are found here, and that in a
situation which I never saw the like of in any part of England;
and, I believe, the like is not to be seen so contrived in any part
of the world; I mean coals and running water upon the tops of
the highest hills: This seems to have been directed by the wise
hand of Providence for the very purpose which is now served by
it, namely, the manufactures, which otherwise could not be
carried on; neither indeed could one-fifth part of the inhabitants be supported without them, for the land could not maintain them. After we had mounted the third hill, we found the
country, in short, one continued village, tho' mountainous
every way, as before; hardly a house standing out of a speaking
distance from another, and (which soon told us their business)
the day clearing up, and the sun shining, we could see that
almost at every house there was a tenter, and almost on every
tenter a piece of cloth, or kersie, or shalloon, for they are the
three articles of that country's labour; from which the sun
glancing, and, as I may say, shining (the white reflecting
its rays) to us, I thought it was the most agreeable sight that
I ever saw, for the hills, as I say, rising and falling so thick,
and the vallies opening sometimes one way, sometimes another,
so that sometimes we could see two or three miles this way,
sometimes as far another; sometimes like the streets near St.
Giles's, called the Seven Dials; we could see through the glades
almost every way round us, yet look which way we would, high

to the tops, and low to the bottoms, it was all the same; innumerable houses and tenters, and a white piece upon every tenter.

But to return to the reason of dispersing the houses, as above; I found, as our road pass'd among them, for indeed no road could do otherwise, wherever we pass'd any house we found a little rill or gutter of running water, if the house was above the road, it came from it, and cross'd the way to run to another; if the house was below us, it cross'd us from some other distant house above it, and at every considerable house was a manufactory or work-house, and as they could not do their business without water, the little streams were so parted and guided by gutters or pipes, and by turning and dividing the streams, that none of those houses were without a river, if I may call it so, running into and through their work-houses.

Again, as the dying-houses, scouring-shops and places where they used this water, emitted the water again, ting'd with the drugs of the dying fat, and with the oil, the soap, the tallow, and other ingredients used by the clothiers in dressing and scouring, &c. which then runs away thro' the lands to the next, the grounds are not only universally watered, how dry soever the season, but that water so ting'd and so fatten'd enriches the lands they run through, that 'tis hardly to be imagined how fertile and rich the soil is made by it.

Then, as every clothier must keep a horse, perhaps two, to fetch and carry for the use of his manufacture, (viz.) to fetch home his wooll and his provisions from the market, to carry his yarn to the spinners, his manufacture to the fulling mill, and, when finished, to the market to be sold, and the like; so every manufacturer generally keeps a cow or two, or more, for his family, and this employs the two, or three, or four pieces of enclosed land about his house, for they scarce sow corn enough for their cocks and hens; and this feeding their grounds still adds by the dung of the cattle, to enrich the soil.

But now, to speak of the bounty of nature again, which I but just mentioned; it is to be observed, that these hills are so furnished by nature with springs and mines, that not only on the sides, but even to the very tops, there is scarce a hill but you find, on the highest part of it, a spring of water, and a coal-pit. I doubt not but there are both springs and coal-pits lower in the hills, 'tis enough to say they are at the top; but, as I say, the hills are so full of springs, so the lower coal-pits may perhaps be too full of water, to work without dreins to carry it off, and the coals in the upper pits being easie to come at, they may chuse to work them, because the horses which fetch the coals, go light up the hill, and come loaden down.

Having thus fire and water at every dwelling, there is no need to enquire why they dwell thus dispers'd upon the highest hills, the convenience of the manufactures requiring it. Among the manufacturers houses are likewise scattered an infinite number of cottages or small dwellings, in which dwell the workmen which are employed, the women and children of whom, are always busy carding, spinning, etc. so that no hands being unemploy'd, all can gain their bread, even from the youngest to the antient; hardly any thing above four years old, but its hands are sufficient to it self.

This is the reason also why we saw so few people without doors; but if we knock'd at the door of any of the master manufacturers, we presently saw a house full of lusty fellows, some at the dye-fat, some dressing the cloths, some in the loom, some one thing, some another, all hard at work, and full employed upon the manufacture, and all seeming to have sufficient business.

I should not have dwelt so upon this part, if there was not abundance of things subsequent to it, which will be explained by this one description, and which are needful to be understood by any one that desires a full understanding of the manner how the people of England are employed, and do subsist in these remoter parts where they are so numerous; for this is one of the most populous parts of Britain, London and the adjacent parts excepted.

. . . it is the opinion of some that know the town, and its

bounds very well, that the number of people in the vicaridge of Hallifax, is encreased one fourth, at least, within the last forty years, that is to say, since the late Revolution. Nor is it improbable at all, for besides the number of houses which are encreased, they have entered upon a new manufacture which was never made in those parts before, at least, not in any quantities, I mean, the manufactures of shalloons, of which they now make, if fame does not bely them, a hundred thousand pieces a year in this parish only, and yet do not make much fewer kersies than they did before.

The trade in kersies also was so great, that I was told by very creditable, honest men, when I was there, men not given to gasconading or boasting, and less to lying, that there was one dealer in the vicaridge, who traded, by commission, for threescore thousand pounds a year in kersies only, and all that to Holland and Hamburgh.

But not to enter into particulars, it is evident that the trade must be exceeding great, in that it employs such a very great number of people, and that in this one town only; for, as I shall fully describe in my account of other places, this is not what I may call the eldest son of the cloathing trade in this county; the town of Leeds challenges a pre-eminence, and I believe, merits the dignity it claims, besides the towns of Huthersfield, Bradforth, Wakefield, and others.

. . . From Hallifax it is twelve miles to Leeds north east, and about as many to Wakefield; due east, or a little southerly, between Hallifax and Leeds, is a little town called Burstall. Here the kersey and shalloon trade being, as it were, confined to Hallifax, and the towns already named, of Huthersfield and Bradforth, they begin to make broad cloth; I call it broad, in distinction from kersies and druggets, and such things, though the cloths in this country are called narrow, when they are spoken of in London, and compared with the broad cloths made in Wilts, Gloucester, Somerset and Devonshire, of which I have spoken in former letters.

This town is famed for dying, and they make a sort of cloths here in imitation of the Gloucester white cloths, bought for the Dutch and the Turkey trades; and though their cloths here may not be as fine, they told us their colours are as good. But that is not my business to dispute, the west country clothiers deny it; and so I leave it as I find it.

From hence to Leeds, and every way to the right hand and the left, the country appears busy, diligent, and even in a hurry of work, they are not scattered and dispersed as in the vicaridge of Hallifax, where the houses stand one by one; but in villages, those villages large, full of houses, and those houses thronged with people, for the whole country is infinitely populous.

A noble scene of industry and application is spread before you here, and which, joined to the market at Leeds, where it chiefly centers, is such a surprising thing, that they who have pretended to give an account of Yorkshire, and have left this out, must betray an ignorance not to be accounted for, or excused; 'tis what is well worth the curiosity of a stranger to go on purpose to see; and many travellers and gentlemen have come over from Hamburgh, nay, even from Leipsick in Saxony, on purpose to see it.

And this brought me from the villages where this manufacture is wrought, to the market where it is sold, which is at Leeds.

Leeds is a large, wealthy and populous town, it stands on the north bank of the river Aire, or rather on both sides the river, for there is a large suburb or part of the town on the south side of the river, and the whole is joined by a stately and prodigiously strong stone bridge, so large, and so wide, that formerly the cloth market was kept in neither part of the town, but on the very bridge it self; and therefore the refreshment given the clothiers by the inn-keepers, of which I shall speak presently, is called the Brigg-shot to this day.

The encrease of the manufacturers and of the trade, soon made the market too great to be confined to the brigg or bridge, and it is now kept in the High-street, beginning from the bridge, and running up north almost to the market-house,

where the ordinary market for provisions begins, which also is
the greatest of its kind in all the north of England, except Hallifax, of which I have spoken already, nay, the people at Leeds
will not allow me to except Hallifax, but say, that theirs is the
greatest market, and that not the greatest plenty only, but the
best of all kinds of provisions are brought hither.

But this is not the case; it is the cloth market I am now to
describe, which is indeed a prodigy of its kind, and is not to be
equalled in the world. The market for serges at Exeter is indeed
a wonderful thing, and the value sold there is very great; but
then the market there is but once a week, here it is twice a week,
and the quantity of goods vastly great too.

The market it self is worth describing, tho' no description can
come up to the thing it self; however, take a sketch of it with its
customs and usages as follows:

The street is a large, broad, fair, and well-built street, beginning, as I have said, at the bridge, and ascending to the
north.

Early in the morning, there are tressels placed in two rows in
the street, sometimes two rows on a side, but always one row
at least; then there are boards laid across those tressels, so that
the boards lie like long counters on either side, from one end of
the street to the other.

The clothiers come early in the morning with their cloth; and
as few clothiers bring more than one piece, the market being so
frequent, they go into the inns and publick-houses with it, and
there set it down.

At seven a clock in the morning, the clothiers being supposed
to be all come by that time, even in the winter, but the hour is
varied as the seasons advance . . . the market bell rings; it
would surprize a stranger to see in how few minutes, without
hurry or noise, and not the least disorder, the whole market is
fill'd; all the boards upon the tressels are covered with cloth,
close to one another as the pieces can lie long ways by one
another, and behind every piece of cloth, the clothier standing
to sell it.

... As soon as the bell has done ringing, the merchants and factors, and buyers of all sorts, come down, and calling along the spaces between the rows of boards, they walk up the rows, and down as their occasions direct. Some of them have their foreign letters of orders, with patterns seal'd on them, in rows, in their hands; and with those they match colours, holding them to the cloths as they think they agree to; when they see any cloths to their colours, or that suit their occasions, they reach over to the clothier and whisper, and in the fewest words imaginable the price is stated; one asks, the other bids; and 'tis agree, or not agree, in a moment.

The merchants and buyers generally walk down and up twice on each side of the rows, and in little more than an hour all the business is done; in less than half an hour you will perceive the cloths begin to move off, the clothier taking it upon his shoulder to carry it to the merchant's house; and by half an hour after eight a clock the market bell rings again; immediately the buyers disappear, the cloth is all sold, or if here and there a piece happens not to be bought, 'tis carried back into the inn, and, in a quarter of an hour, there is not a piece of cloth to be seen in the market.

Thus, you see, ten or twenty thousand pounds value in cloth, and sometimes much more, bought and sold in little more than an hour, and the laws of the market the most strictly observed as ever I saw done in any market in England. . . . Daniel Defoe. *A Tour through the Whole Island of Great Britain*, 3 vols, 1724–6, III

———

Dr John Aikin (1747–1822), the son of a dissenting theologian, was trained as a physician at Edinburgh, London, and Leyden. A friend of the liberal Unitarian Joseph Priestley, he practised in Yarmouth, Stoke Newington, and Warrington. He was also a considerable writer, particularly known for his celebrated account of the Manchester region, which he extended to cover most of the Northern textile areas. In the following extract he describes the subdivisions of the eighteenth-century Yorkshire woollen industry. The domestic clothiers were often praised. 'Any industrious individual possessing credit for a capital of £10', William Wilberforce told the House of Commons in 1800, 'buys therewith a pack of wool, works it up with the assistance of his wife and family, and brings it to the public market for sale, just as the little farmers bring their little articles of produce; the wealth thus acquired and diffused is not obtained at the expense of domestic happiness, but in the enjoyment of it'.

----

4 The whole number of master broad-cloth manufacturers in the West Riding of Yorkshire is about 3240. The mixed cloth manufacturers reside partly in the villages belonging to the parish of Leeds; but chiefly at Morley, Guildersome, Adwalton, Driglington, Pudsey, Farsley, Calverley, Eccleshall, Idle, Baildon, Yeadon, Guisely, Rawdon, and Horsforth, in or bordering upon the vale of Aire, chiefly west of Leeds; and at Batley, Dewsbury, Ossett, Horbury, and Kirkburton, west of Wakefield, in or near the vale of Calder. Not a single manufacturer is to be found more than one mile east, or two north, of Leeds; nor are there many in the town of Leeds, and those only in the outskirts.

The white cloth is manufactured chiefly at Alverthorpe, Ossett, Kirkheaton, Dewsbury, Batley, Birstal, Hopton, Mirfield, Archet, Clackheaton, Littletown, Bowling and Shipley; a tract of country forming an oblique belt across the hills that separate the vale of Calder from the vale of Aire, beginning about a mile west of Wakefield, leaving Huddersfield and Bradford a little to the left, terminating at Shipley on the Aire, and not coming within less than about six miles of Leeds on the right. The districts of the white and coloured cloth manufactory are generally distinct, but are a little intermixed at the south-east and north-west extremities.

The cloths are sold in their respective halls rough as they come from the fulling mills. They are finished by the merchants, who employ dressers, dyers, &c., for that purpose; these, with

drysalters, shop-keepers, and the different kind of handicrafts-
men common to every town, compose the bulk of the inhabitants of Leeds. The dispersed state of the manufactures in
villages and single houses over the whole face of the country, is
highly favourable to their morals and happiness. They are
generally men of small capitals, and often annex a small farm
to their other business; great numbers of the rest have a field or
two to support a horse and a cow, and are for the most part
blessed with the comforts, without the superfluities, of life.
John Aikin. *A Description of the Country from thirty to forty miles
round Manchester*, 1795, 573–4

Sir Edward Baines (1800–1890), second son of the celebrated
Edward Baines (1774–1848), the Congregationalist owner-
editor of the Liberal *Leeds Mercury*, was a politician (as MP for
Leeds in 1859–74), journalist, propagandist, and versatile
author. In addition to a large number of polemical tracts, he
published major works on Northern history and industry. The
following brief extract helps to explain the difference between
the woollen and worsted industries. It is taken from a paper
read before the British Association for the Advancement of
Science at its Leeds meeting in 1858. Baines's brother Thomas
(1806–81) republished it in his monumental history of Yorkshire in 1870. Thomas was editor of the *Liverpool Times*, a
Parliamentary agent, and a Northern historian.

5 . . . But the essential distinction of woollens from worsted,
cotton, linen, and every other textile fabric is, that they depend
upon that peculiar property of sheep's wool, its disposition to
felt; that is, under pressure and warm moisture, to *interlock its
fibres* as by strong mutual attraction, and thus to *run up* into a
compact substance not easily separable. Wools differ in the
degree of this felting property; but, generally speaking, the long
wools possess it in a lower degree than the short wools, and the
wools which felt best are the best adapted for making woollen
cloth. For worsted stuffs the felting property is not required;

and not only have the wools used for this purpose less of the felting property, but they are so treated in the spinning and manufacture as almost entirely to destroy it.

In every other textile fabric, when the material is spun into yarn and woven into a web, the fabric is complete. But in woollen cloth, after the process of spinning and weaving comes the essential process of felting, by means of heavy pressure with soap and warm water; and so efficacious is this process, that a piece of cloth under it often shrinks up to two-thirds its original length and little more than half its width. . . .   Edward Baines. 'The Woollen Manufacture of England; with special reference to the Leeds Clothing District', in Thomas Baines. *Yorkshire, Past and Present: A History and a Description of the Three Ridings of the Great County of York* . . . 2 vols, 1870, I, 629–30

———

The worsted industry of medieval Yorkshire waned in Tudor times and began a slow return to the county in the late seventeenth century. During the late eighteenth century Yorkshire worsteds gradually overtook Norwich production, particularly when Northern masters adopted the new machinery designed for the cotton industry and established the early spinning mills. Bradford and Halifax became the new centres of the expanding industry, the former town eventually taking the lead. Worsted cloth, depending upon the strength of the thread rather than on the interlocking of the material through felting, was generally made of the longer fibres, which were 'arranged' by the combing process (while the shorter fibres intended for the woollen manufacture were mingled by carding). John James (1811–67), the Bradford antiquarian, here gives his version of the vital period in the industry's history when its base moved from Norfolk to Yorkshire.

———

6   A period has now been approached, the latter half of the eighteenth century, in which our manufactures from wool experienced a remarkable development, especially in Yorkshire.

In this interval, the worsted branch of industry seems peculiarly to have flourished, furnishing subsistence to thousands of the poor. But its principal extension took place in the West-Riding of Yorkshire, where in the year 1774, the value of the manufacture amounted to the immense sum of £1,400,000; here also, before the termination of the century, the inventions of spinning machines were first applied to the production of worsted yarn, and were destined ere long to produce such a remarkable transformation and growth in all the departments of the trade.

But to return. During the middle of the eighteenth century the manufacturers of Norwich attained the greatest prosperity. The Norwich merchants and tradesmen being energetic and fertile in resources, when one market, or branch of business failed, turned to another. Finding that the monopoly which they had to a great extent enjoyed in the home demand, had, through the competition in cotton goods, vanished, they directed their attention more to foreign markets, and soon by increased exports obtained compensation for the loss they had sustained from this cause. So true it is that monopolies create supineness and sluggishness in commerce, whilst competition stimulates to exertion and prosperity. Between the years 1743 to that of 1763, Norwich reached the palmy, the highest state of its greatness, as 'the chief seat of the chief manufacture of the realm'. Undoubtedly in those times it occupied, as 'the chief seat of manufacture', the position of the present Manchester.

Two places in England then stood distinguished for the excellence of their dyers, London and Norwich, and there most of the fine worsted goods underwent the processes of dyeing and finishing. The workmen of the latter city were pre-eminently known for the beauty and permanence of their dyes. Worsted textures were forwarded thither from all parts of England, to be dyed and finished, thus furnishing employment to a large number of workmen, and increasing the trade of the city. . . .

. . . In the ten years succeeding the year 1750, the production of stuffs waxed greatly in the West-Riding. Throughout many

districts, where until lately the making of the coarse cloths of
Yorkshire formed the occupation of the majority of the population, the clothiers engaged, with energy, in the comparatively
new business of stuff-making. Halifax and Bradford much extended their operations therein, and even at Leeds, the very
centre of the clothing country, the weaving of worsteds constituted no inconsiderable portion of its trade. Merchants had
in abundance sprung up, who rode from town to town, and
valley to valley, to purchase these goods, which were mostly
shipped to the continent of Europe. A new road to wealth had
been opened—the farmer either forsook the tilling of the
ground to follow altogether the stuff business, or else carried it
on as a domestic employment along with the cultivation of the
land, and with thrifty habits, was often in an incredibly short
time, enabled to purchase his homestead and farm. The art
spread into the most remote dells, as well as in the towns and
villages of the south-western portion of the Riding. All ranks
hastened to learn, in some of its branches, the worsted business
—some as sorters, others as combers, more as weavers, whilst
the women and children were taught spinning, and for the
instruction and employment of the latter, numerous schools for
teaching spinning were established. Although the art of making
stuffs had been practised in the Riding to a considerable extent
since at least the commencement of the century, yet in the
interval between the years 1750 and 1760, a new era opened,
and from that point the manufacture began to exhibit some
indications of that stature and dimensions which, in later days,
it has attained. It, year by year, increased. Large quantities of
northern made stuffs were shipped to Holland by way of Hull.
In the year 1765, about one thousand packs of the produce of
Yorkshire and Norfolk looms, were imported at Rotterdam.*
To Spain also, and Portugal, Yorkshire stuffs were exported in

---

* In 1765, the Exports of Manufactures from Wool to Holland, amounted
to above £320,000. It is stated, that at this period, serges to the value of
£10,000 were sent to Holland from Aberdeenshire, so that the Scotch
worsted weavers still to some extent competed with us there.

C

considerable amounts, and likewise to America by way of Liverpool.

In Norwich, likewise, at the commencement of the reign of George III, the worsted manufacture continued in a vigorous and thriving state. On the failure, to a great extent, as before noticed, of the home demand for Norwich crapes and goods, the stuff merchants cultivated the export trade more than formerly, and now transacted a very extensive business in Holland, Flanders, Germany, Italy, Spain and Portugal, (and through them to the great markets of South America,) where they established agents and correspondents, and employed numerous travellers, as well often taking journies thither themselves. . . .

The East India Company also purchased largely of Norwich goods, such as camblets, and in particular their purchases, owing to the stoppage of French commerce to the East from the war, increased very greatly in the year 1762. But the prosperity of Norwich, soon after the accession of George III, began to decline. This was partly owing to the rapid increase of the Yorkshire manufacture, and partly owing to the war which broke out between England and her American colonies. The merchants, in fear of the privateers, lessened their exports, and commerce became crippled. . . . John James, *History of the Worsted Manufacture in England, from the Earliest Times: with Introductory Notices of the Manufacture among the Ancient Nations, and during the Middle Ages*, 1857, 258–9, 267–9   _____

The Southern Woollen Industries   For many centuries of English history woollen manufacture was agriculture's nearest rival as an industry and a source of employment. It was always widely spread, and particular districts eventually earned reputations for specialised production; the West Country in general had a name for high-quality work. On the eve of the Industrial Revolution, Arthur Young visited and described some of the old centres of woollen production.

[24 June 1767]

7 From *Hadleigh* I continued my journey to *Sudbury*, an exceeding dirty, but a great manufacturing town. I made such
enquiries as were most likely to acquire some good information
relative to their manufactures; and my intelligence ran as
follows: they possess a great number of hands, who earn their
livelihood by working up the wool from the sheep's back to the
weaving it into says and burying-crape, which are their principal articles. The spinning is here a poor business; a stout girl of
15 or 16, not being able to earn above 6*d*. a day; but the combing is the best of all their employments, yielding from 12*s*. to
14*s*. a week; the weavers of the says and burying-crape earn
from 7*s*. to 9*s*. but the first price the most common; besides
these articles they weave ship-flags, which employ the women,
and girls of seven or eight years of age, yielding the latter about
2*s*. 6*d*. or 3*s*. a week. The whole manufactory works chiefly for
the *London* markets; but some says go down their river (which is
navigable hence to *Maningtree*) for exportation.

[2 July 1767]

Witney is very famous for its woollen manufactory; which
consists of what they call kersey pieces, coarse bear-skins, and
blankets. The two first they make for the *North American* market;
vast quantities being sent up the river St. *Lawrence*, and likewise to *New-York*. Their finest blankets, which rise in price to
3 *l*. a pair, are exported to *Spain* and *Portugal*; but all are sent to
London first in broad-wheel waggons, of which, four or five go
every week. The finest wools they work, come from *Herefordshire*
and *Worcestershire*, and sell from 8*d*. to 10*d*. a pound. The
coarsest from *Lincolnshire*; they call it dag-locks; they sell for 4½*d*.
per lb. and are used for making the coarse bear-skins. There are
above 500 weavers in this town, who work up 7000 packs of
wool annually. Journeymen in general, on an average, earn
from 10*s*. to 12*s*. a week, all the year round, both summer and
winter; but they work from four to eight, and in winter by
candle-light; the work is of that nature, that a boy of fourteen

earns as much as a man. One of seven or eight earns by quilling
and cornering, 1*s*. 6*d*. and 1*s*. 8*d*. a week, and girls the same.
Old women of 60 and 70 earn 6*d*. a day in picking and sorting
the wool: a good stout woman can earn from 10*d* to 1*s*. a day by
spinning; and a girl of 14, four pence or five pence. They weave
according to the season; in winter kerseys and bear-skins ready
for shipping in the summer up the St. *Lawrence*; and in summer
blankets for home consumption, and *Spain* and *Portugal*. One
remarkable circumstance is, that none of the manufacturers
ever work for the farmers. The blankets usually purchased at
home, are about 23*s*. or 24*s*. a pair, ten quarters wide and
twelve long; and the corners are wrought for a halfpenny a
piece.

[13 July 1767]

As to manufactures, there are considerable ones of flannels
and linseys at *Salisbury*; at which the journeymen earn from 7*s*.
to 9*s*. a week the year round: and at *Romsey*, near 500 hands are
employed in making those shalloons which are called Ratinetts:
the journeymen earn, on an average, 9*s*. a week all the year;
and a girl of sixteen or eighteen, a shilling a day by weaving,
but in the neighbouring village, by spinning, not above half as
much; the children are employed at quilting very young.
Arthur Young. *A Six Weeks Tour, through the Southern Counties
of England and Wales*, 1768, 58–9, 99—101, 171

A Mercantile Community   Under the varied 'domestic
systems', the merchants who formed the peak of the social
pyramid in eighteenth-century industrial areas became a
dominant group. In the old market towns they often dominated
an hierarchical society by establishing their own oligarchic control of local institutions. Before the reform of the municipal
corporations in 1835, they exercised a paternalistic and generally benevolent rule in such towns as Leeds, the largest Yorkshire
woollen centre. The following paragraphs describe the growth
of the town during the eighteenth-century expansion of local
industry.

8   All the early prosperity of Leeds . . . sprang from its trade in woollen goods; yet in the middle of the [eighteenth] century . . . this trade was still in its infancy. Leeds itself was, in comparison with its present condition, an insignificant town, hardly longer than the length of Briggate, stretching westward no further than Trinity Church, and with Saint Peter's Church for almost its eastern limit. Saint John's Church, with the Free Grammar School and Harrison's Almshouses adjoining, formed its [northern] boundary; and all the town was contained on the northern side of the Aire. The old Norman bridge at the foot of Briggate still sufficed for the weekly cloth-market; the traders of the town and the country manufacturers being called together by a bell wrung in the quaint bridge-chapel, and the merchants of Hull, Boston, and similar places coming there to buy the cloths and carry them away in river-boats.

By 1758, however, the trade had outgrown that old-fashioned mart, and, accordingly, a commodious building, now known as the Mixed Cloth Hall, was set up a little to the west of Trinity Church. This structure, thought preposterously large at the time of its erection, formed a quadrangle three hundred and sixty-four feet long, and a hundred and ninety-two feet broad, with an inner court measuring three hundred and thirty feet, by ninety-six. It was accessible by seven doors, was lighted by a hundred and sixty-seven windows, and was large enough, it was reckoned, to hold 109,200 *l*'s worth of cloth at a time. Within seventeen years from its opening, it was found necessary to build another meeting-place. The White Cloth Hall, between Briggate and Saint Peter's Church, was completed in 1775; and within a few years, nine similar structures were opened in all the trading towns of the West Riding of Yorkshire. All grew with the growth of Leeds. In 1775, Leeds contained 17,117 inhabitants. By 1801 the population had increased to 30,699; in 1821 it amounted to 83,746; and in 1865 it was estimated at 224,025.

. . . Most of the wool was made into cloth by small manu-

facturers scattered about the country, and lodged in the different towns and villages of the West Riding. These manufacturers brought or sent their goods to the markets of such places
as Leeds, Bradford, or Wakefield, there either to be sold at
once to the wholesale merchants, who came from other parts
of England or from foreign countries, or to be collected by the
wool-staplers and reserved for subsequent distribution. There
were no manufactures conducted on the extensive scale now
common, and necessary to the more finished workmanship of
modern times, until Benjamin Gott set the fashion. H. R. Fox
Bourne. *English Merchants: Memoirs in Illustration of the Progress
of English Commerce*, 1866, II, 217–18, 219

The Lancashire Cotton Industry The greatest and most
famous of nineteenth-century British industries, the Lanca-
shire-dominated production of cotton goods, had a long history.
Although much of the cloth was finished in London, the domestic industry had for long been concentrated in Lancashire,
where cotton slowly took the lead from wool and then rapidly
expanded beyond the county. In the family division of labour,
the man would weave and the women and children card and
spin. Edward Baines here gives a Victorian view and interpre-
tation of the early history of the industry, before a long series of
inventions revolutionised production during the eighteenth
century. Raw cotton imports rose from 1,396,000lb in 1700
to 56,011,000 in 1800.

----

9 The exact period when the cotton manufacture was introduced into England is unknown. The article of cotton-wool had
for centuries been imported in small quantities, to be used as
candle-wicks, as appears from an entry in the books of Bolton
abbey, in Yorkshire, in the year 1298—"In sapo et *cotoun* ad
candelam, xvii s. id."* The next mention of cotton-wool that I

----

* Dr. Whitaker's History of Craven, p. 384 (2d edition, 1812). This antiquarian, whose prejudices against manufactures were violent and ridiculous,
says, in a note on the above extract—"This substance, (cotton,) of which

have met with, is in "The Processe of the Libel of English Policie", . . . originally published in 1430, and republished in Hakluyt's Collection of early Voyages: the trade of the Genoese with England is thus described:

"The Genuois comen in sundry wies
Into this land by diuers merchandises
In great Caracks, arrayed withouten lacke
With cloth of gold, silke, and pepper blacke
They bring with them, and of crood† great plentee,
Woll Oyle, Woad ashen, by vessel in the see,
Cotton, Rochalum, and good gold of Genne;
And then be charged with wolle again I wenne,
And wollen cloth of ours of colours all."

At the beginning of the sixteenth century, the evidences of a regular importation of cotton become more numerous. Hakluyt records that "in the yeeres of our Lord 1511, 1512, &c. till the year 1534, diuers tall ships of London, [he mentions five,] with certaine other ships of Southampton and Bristow, had an ordinary and usual trade to Sicilia, Candie, Chio, and some-whiles to Cyprus, as also to Tripolis and Barutti, in Syria. The commodities which they carried thither were, fine kersies of diuers colours, course kersies, white Westerne dozens, cottons, [no doubt, strong woollens,] certain clothes called statutes, and others called cardinal-whites, and calneskins, which were well sold in Sicilie, &c. The commodities which they brought backe were silks, chamlets, rubarbe, malmesies, muskudels and other wines, sweete oyles, *cotten wool*, Turkie carpets, galles, pepper, cinnamon, and some other spices".*

. . . It is evident that cotton wool had long been in use, but, in all probability, it was only for candle-wicks, and other minor purposes, not at all for the manufacture of cloth. No mention

the manufactory is become so extensive and so pernicious, was then imported in small quantities from the Levant".
† Woad.
* Hakluyt, vol. ii. p. 206.

has yet been found of the cotton manufacture earlier than the year 1641; and there are good reasons for concluding that it could not have existed very long before that period. . . .

In the year 1582, a commercial treaty having been formed with Turkey, and a Levant company established, a mercantile commission was sent from London to Constantinople and other parts of Turkey, to learn any secrets in manufacturing and dyeing that might be useful to the domestic industry and foreign trade of England, and thus tend to give employment to "our poor people withall, and promote the general enriching of this realme". . . . If the cotton manufacture had then been practised in England, even on a small scale, it is highly probable that this commission would have received directions either to observe the processes of the manufacture in the East, or to inquire concerning the supply of the raw material.

It is not impossible that this very commission, acting on the general principle of its instructions, might bring to England the art of making cotton cloth. But I am more inclined to think that the art was imported from Flanders, about the same time, by the crowd of Protestant artisans and workmen who fled from Antwerp, on the capture and ruin of that great trading city by the duke of Parma in 1585; and also from other cities of the Spanish Netherlands. Great numbers of these victims of a sanguinary persecution took refuge in England, and some of them settled in Manchester; and there is the stronger reason to suppose that the manufacture of cotton would then be commenced here, as there were restrictions and burdens on foreigners setting up business as masters in England, in the trades then carried on in this country, whilst foreigners commencing a *new* art would be exempt from those restrictions.* The warden and fellows of Manchester college had the wisdom to encourage the settlement of the foreign clothiers in that town, by allowing them to cut firing from their extensive woods, as well as to take the timber necessary for the construction of their looms, on paying the small sum of four-pence yearly.

* Macpherson's Annals of Commerce, vol. ii. p. 176.

At that period of our history, when capital was small, and the movements of trade comparatively sluggish, a new manufacture would be likely to extend itself slowly, and to be long before it attracted the notice of authors. That a manufacture might in those days gradually take root and acquire strength, without even for half a century being commemorated in any book that should be extant after the lapse of two centuries more, will be easily credited by those who have searched for the records of our modern improvements in the same manufacture. If the greatest mechanical inventions and the most stupendous commercial phenomena have passed almost unnoticed in a day when authors were so numerous, the mere infancy of the cotton manufacture may well have been without record in an age when the press was far less active.

We may decisively infer from the first mention that has been discovered of the cotton manufacture in England, that it had been growing up for a considerable time before that account was written. This passage, memorable in the history of the manufacture, is found in a little work by Lewes Roberts, called "The Treasure of Traffic", published in 1641. It is as follows:

"The town of Manchester, in Lancashire, (says he,) must be also herein remembered, and worthily for their encouragement commended, who buy the yarne of the Irish in great quantity, and, weaving it, returne the same again into Ireland to sell: Neither doth their industry rest here, for they buy *cotton wool* in London, that comes first from Cyprus and Smyrna, and at home worke the same, and perfect it into *fustians, vermillions, dimities,* and other such stuffes, and then return it to London, where the same is vented and sold, and not seldom sent into forrain parts, who have means, at far easier termes, to provide themselves of the said first materials." (Orig. Edition, pp. 32, 33.)

The same author further says—

"The Levant or Turkey Company brings in return thereof (i.e. of English woollens) great quantity of *Cotten* and *Cotten-yarne,* Grogram yarne, and raw silke into England, (which shewes the benefit accruing to this kingdom by that Company);

for here the said cloth is first shipped out and exported in its full perfection, dyed and drest, and thereby the prime native commoditie of this kingdom is increased, improved, and vented, and the cotten yarne and raw silk obtained." (p. 34.)

From the above evidence it is manifest that the cotton manufacture had in 1641 become well established at Manchester. It not only then supplied the home trade with several kinds of cotton goods, but furnished them as a regular article of exportation from the metropolis to the distant markets of the Levant; and the importation of cotton-wool and cotton-yarn had also become regular and considerable. Manchester still retained its manufacture of linen; and as linen-yarn was used as the warp for fustians and nearly all other cotton goods in this country down to the year 1773, it may be said that the linen manufacture prepared the way for the cotton manufacture, and long continued its auxiliary. It may, therefore, from all the above facts, be regarded as in a very high degree probable, that the cotton manufacture was introduced into England towards the close of the sixteenth century, by the Flemish protestant emigrants.

. . . The spread of the manufacture was afterwards by no means rapid. The same obstacles which impeded its growth in the other countries of Europe, impeded it in England. Owing to the rudeness of the spinning machinery, fine yarn could not be spun, and of course fine goods could not be woven. Fustians, dimities, and other strong fabrics were made; but calicoes and the more delicate cotton goods were not attempted.

. . . At this period, the extent of mercantile establishments, and the modes of doing business, were extremely different from what they are at present. Though a few individuals are found who made fortunes by trade, it is probable that the capital of merchants was generally very small, until the end of the seventeenth century, and all their concerns were managed with extreme frugality. Masters commonly participated in the labours of their servants. Commercial enterprise was exceedingly limited. Owing to the bad state of the roads, and the

entire absence of inland navigation, goods could only be con-
veyed on pack-horses, with a gang of which the Manchester
chapmen used occasionally to make circuits to the principal
towns, and sell their goods to the shopkeepers,—bringing back
with them sheep's wool, which was disposed of to the makers of
worsted yarn at Manchester, or to the clothiers of Rochdale,
Saddleworth, and the West Riding of Yorkshire. It was only
towards the close of the seventeenth century, that trade became
sufficiently productive to encourage the general erection of
brick houses in Manchester, in place of the old dwellings, constructed of wood and plaster. So great was the increase of the
manufactures and trade of England towards the close of this
century, that the exports rose from £2,022,812, in 1662, (and
they were about the same in 1668,) to £6,788,166, in 1699.*

In the latter part of the seventeenth century and the beginning of the eighteenth, such considerable importations of
Indian calicoes, muslins, and chintzes were made, as to excite
the vehement opposition of our manufacturers, and to lead
parliament to exclude those goods by heavy penalties. . . . The
jealousy felt in England was not, however, on behalf of our
cotton manufacture, but of our woollen and silk manufactures;
which sufficiently proves that no cotton goods were then made
in England of the fine and light qualities of those from
India.

The business of calico printing was commenced in London
in the latter part of the seventeenth century; and for the sake
of encouraging this branch of industry, plain Indian calicoes
were admitted under a duty. In 1712, the business had become
sufficiently extensive to lead parliament to impose an excise
duty of 3d. per square yard on calicoes printed, stained,
painted, or dyed, (10 Anne, c. 19.); and in 1714, the duty was
raised to 6d. per square yard, (12 Anne, sec. 2, c. 9.). . . .

In the twenty years from 1720 to 1740, which was a period
of almost uninterrupted peace, Manchester, as well as many

* Dr. Davenant's Report to the Commissioners of Accounts; and Anderson's
Origin and History of Commerce, vol. II. pp. 227, 228.

other commercial towns, continued to make rapid strides in wealth, population, and manufacturing eminence.

Dr. Stukely, who visited Manchester about 1720, says, in his *Itinerarium Curiosum*,—"The trade, which is incredibly large, consists much in fustians, girth-webb, tukings, tapes, &c., which are dispersed all over the kingdom, and to foreign parts."

Daniel de Foe, in his "*Tour through the whole Island of Great Britain*", published in 1727, speaking of Manchester, says, "That within a very few years past, here, as at Liverpoole, and also at Froome in Somersetshire, the town is extended in a surprising manner, being almost double to what it was a few years ago. So that, taking in all its suburbs, it now contains at least 50,000 people. [This must have included the whole parish.] The grand manufacture which has so much raised this town is that of *cotton* in all its varieties, which, like all our other manufactures, is very much increased within these thirty or forty years".*

De Foe says also, "About eight miles from Manchester, N.W., lies Bolton. We saw nothing remarkable in it, but that the cotton manufacture reached hither, though the place did not, like Manchester, seem increasing. . . ."

As linen yarn was used for the warps of cotton goods, the progress of the cotton manufacture increased the demand for linen yarn to such an extent as to inconvenience the linen weavers of Scotland and Ireland, who complained of the yarn being bought out of their hands, at a high price, to be sent to Manchester, and there wrought up with cottons. . . .

An article in the *Daily Advertiser*, of September 5, 1739, and which was also copied into the *Gentleman's Magazine*, says—"The manufacture of *cotton*, mixed and plain, is arrived at so great perfection within these twenty years, that we not only make enough for our own consumption, but supply our colonies, and many of the nations of Europe. The benefits arising from this branch are such as to enable the manufacturers of Manchester

* De Foe's Tour, Vol. III. p. 219.

alone to lay out above thirty thousand pounds a year, for many years past, on additional buildings. 'Tis computed, that two thousand new houses have been built in that industrious town within these twenty years."

In a rapidly advancing country, the great things of one age are insignificant in the eyes of the succeeding age. Thus, the period of 1739, whose prosperity was so much vaunted, is now looked back upon as the mere feeble infancy of the cotton manufacture—a trickling rill, compared with the mighty river to which that manufacture has since swelled. At that time the consumption of cotton wool did not exceed 1-200th part of the consumption at the present day. . . .

. . . In all probability, Postlethwayt, the author of the 'Universal Dictionary of Trade and Commerce', approached to correctness, when, in the year 1766, he estimated the annual value of the cottons made at £600,000. He says—"The manufactures called Manchester wares, such as fustians, cottons, tapes, incle, &c. are sent on pack-horses to London, Bristol, Liverpool, &c. for exportation, and also to the wholesale haberdashers for home consumption; whence the other towns of England are likewise served, or by the Manchester men themselves, who travel from town to town throughout the kingdom. Of these goods they make, at Manchester, Bolton, and the neighbouring places, above £600,000 annually."

The following return of the quantities of cotton wool imported and exported, is taken from a report of a committee of the house of commons on the linen manufacture, published in Postlethwayt's Dictionary, under the head "Linen" [see next page] :–

In the year 1701, when the exportation of cotton goods did not exceed £23,253 (which appears to have been above the average for the next forty years,) the exportation of woollen goods (according to Dr. Davenant and Mr. Gregory King) amounted to £2,000,000, forming above a fourth of the whole export trade of the kingdom. So great has been the change in the relative proportions of these manufactures, that, whilst the

COTTON WOOL IMPORTED AND EXPORTED

Years	Imported lbs.	Exported lbs.	Retained for home consumption lbs.
1743	1,132,288	40,870	1,091,418
1744	1,882,873	182,765	1,700,108
1745	1,469,523	73,172	1,369,351
1746	2,264,808	73,279	2,191,529
1747	2,224,869	29,438	2,195,431
1748	4,852,966	291,717	4,561,249
1749	1,658,365	330,998	1,327,367

Compare the above official returns of imports and exports, for the first half of the 18th century, with the present imports of cotton wool and exports of cotton manufactures:

COTTON WOOL IMPORTED IN 1833
303,726,199 lbs.
BRITISH COTTON MANUFACTURES EXPORTED IN 1833
Real or Declared Value
£18,486,400

woollen exports have increased only to £6,539,731 in 1833, the cotton exports amounted in the same year to £18,486,400. The woollen manufacture has continued to extend, but its rate of increase bears no proportion to that of the cotton manufacture, which mocks all that the most romantic imagination could have previously conceived possible under any circumstances. Edward Baines. *History of the Cotton Manufacture in Great Britain*, 1835, 95–102, 105–12

William Radcliffe (1760–1841) was one of the pioneer entrepreneurs of cotton's industrial revolution. As a child he learned to card and spin, before graduating as a weaver and eventually setting up a manufacturing business in Stockport. Aided by Thomas Johnson, in 1804 he constructed a dressing-machine to prepare yarn for power weaving and also patented improved power-looms. His business ability, however, did not match his inventive talent, and his firm collapsed. In the following extract from his largely autobiographical book Radcliffe describes the late eighteenth-century expansion of the cotton industry.

———

10   In the year 1770, the land in our township was occupied by between fifty to sixty farmers; rents, to the best of my recollection, did not exceed 10s. per statute acre; and out of these fifty or sixty farmers, there were only six or seven who raised their rents directly from the produce of their farms; all the rest got their rent partly in some branch of trade, such as spinning and weaving woollen, linen, or cotton. The cottagers were employed entirely in this manner, except for a few weeks in the harvest. Being one of those cottagers, and intimately acquainted with all the rest, as well as every farmer, I am better able to relate particularly how the change from the old system of hand labour to the new one of machinery operated in raising the price of land. Cottage rents at that time, with convenient loom-shop, and a small garden attached, were from one and a half to two guineas per annum. The father of a family would earn from eight shillings to half-a-guinea at his loom; and his sons, if he had one, two, or three alongside of him, six or eight shillings each per week: but the great sheet-anchor of all cottages and small farms, was the labour attached to the hand-wheel; and when it is considered that it required six to eight hands to prepare and spin yarn, of any of the three materials I have mentioned, sufficient for the consumption of one weaver,—this shews clearly the inexhaustible source there was for labour for every person from the age of seven to eighty years, (who retained their sight and could move their hands,) to earn their bread, say one to three shillings per week, without going to the parish. . . .

From the year 1770 to 1788, a complete change had gradually been effected in the spinning of yarns; that of wool had disappeared altogether, and that of linen was also nearly gone:

cotton, cotton, cotton, was become the almost universal
material for employment; the hand-wheels with the exception
of one establishment were all thrown into lumber-rooms; the
yarn was all spun on common jennies; the carding for all
numbers up to 40 hanks in the pound was done on carding
engines; but the finer numbers of 60 to 80 were still carded by
hand, it being a general opinion at that time that machine-
carding would never answer for fine numbers. In weaving, no
great alteration had taken place during these eighteen years,
save the introduction of the fly-shuttle, a change in the woollen
looms to fustians and calico, and the linen nearly gone, except
the few fabrics in which there was a mixture of cotton. To the
best of my recollection, there was no increase of looms during
this period,—but rather a decrease. . . .

. . . The next fifteen years, viz. from 1788 to 1803, . . . I will
call the golden age of this great trade, which has been ever
since in a gradual decline. Water twist and common jenny
yarns had been freely used in Bolton, &c., for some years prior
to 1788; but it was the introduction of mule yarns about this
time, along with the other yarns, all assimilating together and
producing every description of clothing, from the finest book
muslin, lace, stocking, &c., to the heaviest fustian, that gave
such a preponderating wealth through the loom.

. . . These families, up to the time I have been speaking of,
whether as cottagers or small farmers, had supported themselves by the different occupations I have mentioned in spinning
and manufacturing, as their progenitors from the earliest institutions of society had done before them. But the mule twist
now coming into vogue, for the warp, as well as weft, added to
the water-twist and common jenny yarns, with an increasing
demand for every fabric the loom could produce, put all hands
in request, of every age and description. The fabrics made from
wool or linen vanished, while the old loom-shops being insufficient, every lumber-room, even old barns, cart-houses, and
out-buildings of any description, were repaired, windows broke
through the old blank walls, and all fitted up for loom-shops.

This source of making room being at length exhausted, new weavers' cottages, with loom-shops, rose up in every direction; all immediately filled, and, when in full work, the weekly circulation of money, as the price of labour only, rose to five times the amount ever before experienced in this district, every family bringing home weekly 40, 60, 80, 100, or even 120 shillings per week! It may be easily conceived, that this sudden increase of the circulating medium would, in a few years, not only show itself in affording all the necessaries and comforts of life these families might require, but also be felt by those who, abstractedly speaking, might be considered disinterested spectators; but in reality they were not so, for all felt it, and that in the most agreeable way, too; for this money in its peregrinations left something in the pockets of every stone-mason, carpenter, slater, plasterer, glazier, joiner, &c.; as well as the corn-dealer, cheese-monger, butcher, and shopkeepers of every description. The farmers participated as much as any class, by the prices they obtained for their corn, butter, eggs, fowls, with every other article the soil or farm-yard could produce, all of which advanced at length to nearly three times the former price. Nor was the portion of this wealth inconsiderable that found its way into the coffers of the Cheshire squires, who had estates in this district, the rents of their farms being doubled, and in many instances trebled. William Radcliffe. *Origin of the New System of Manufacture commonly called 'Power-Loom Weaving'*, Stockport, 1828, 59–66

The Hosiery Industry The English hosiery industry was traditionally concentrated in the counties of Nottingham, Derby and Leicester, where William Lee's sixteenth-century stocking-frame was widely employed. The stockingers were well organised, moderately prosperous, and 'respectable'; during their struggles against mechanisation they earned the political and financial support of several members of the Midlands aristocracy and gentry. Jedediah Strutt (1726–97), the second son of a dissenting Derbyshire farmer, was trained as a wheel-

D

wright at Findern, near Derby, and later inherited an uncle's farm. He started a revolution in the industry by inventing the 'Derby rib machine' to knit ribbed hosiery. A patent of 1759 gave him a notable lead and founded his fortune. A subsequent partnership with Richard Arkwright led to the development of the Midlands cotton industry and the 'social' rise of the Strutts; Jedediah's eldest son, William (1756–1830) was a Fellow of the Royal Society, and William's son, Edward (1801–80) was created Lord Belper in 1856. Dr Andrew Ure (1778–1857) here sketches the early history of the industry.

---

11   The stocking-frame, to any one who attentively considers its complex operations, and the elegant sleight with which it forms its successive rows of loops or stitches, will appear to be the most extraordinary single feat,—the most remarkable stride, ever made in mechanical invention. In the Stocking Weavers' Hall, in Red Cross Street, London, there is a portrait of a man, painted in the act of pointing to an iron stocking-frame, and addressing a woman, who is knitting with needles by hand. The picture bears the following quaint inscription:— "In the year 1589, the ingenious William Lee, A.M., of St. John's College, Cambridge, devised this profitable art for stockings, (but being despised, went to France,) yet of iron to himself, but to us and to others, of gold; in memory of whom this is here painted".

It was only twenty-eight years prior to the construction of this machine, that the art of knitting stockings, by wires worked by the fingers, had been introduced into England from Spain.

According to one story, Lee was expelled from the University for marrying contrary to the statutes. Having no other means of subsistence, he and his wife were obliged to live on her earnings as a stocking-knitter; when, under the pressure of want, Lee contrived his frame as a method of multiplying production.

But the following is probably a more correct account of the origin of this contrivance. According to an ancient tradition in the neighbourhood of Lee's birth-place,* the stocking-frame was meditated under the inspiration of love, and constructed in consequence of its disappointment. Lee is said to have been in early youth enamoured of a fair mistress of the knitting craft, who had become rich by employing a number of young women at this highly-prized and lucrative industry. The young scholar, after studying fondly the dexterous movements of the lady's hand, had become himself not only an adept in the art, but had imagined a scheme of making artificial fingers for knitting many loops at once. Whether this feminine accomplishment excited jealousy, or detracted from his manly attractions, is not said; but his suit was received with coldness, and then rejected with scorn.

Revenge now prompted him to realize the ideas which love had first inspired. He devoted his days and nights to the construction of the stocking-frame, and brought it, ere long, to such perfection, that it has remained nearly as he left it, without receiving any essential improvement. Having taught its use to his brother and the rest of his relations, he established his frame at Culverton, near Nottingham, as a formidable competitor of female handiwork, teaching his mistress, by the insignificance to which he reduced the implements of her pride, that the love of a man of genius was not to be slighted with impunity.

After practising this business during five years, he had become aware of its importance in a national point of view, and brought his invention to London to seek protection and encouragement from the Court, by whom his fabrics were much admired. The period of his visit was not propitious. Elizabeth, the patroness of whatever ministered to her vanity as a woman, and her state as a princess, was in the last stage of her decline. Her successor was too deeply engrossed with political intrigues for securing the stability of his throne, to be able to afford any leisure for cherishing an infant manufacture. Nay, though Lee and his brother made a pair of stockings in the presence of the King, it

* Woodborough, seven miles from Nottingham.

is said that he viewed their frame rather as a dangerous innovation, likely to deprive the poor of labour and bread, than as a
means of multiplying the resources of national industry, and of
giving profitable employment to many thousand people.

The encouragement to English ingenuity which the narrow-
minded pedant, James, refused, was offered by Henry IV, and
his sagacious minister, Sully. They invited Lee to come to
France with his admirable machines. Thither, accordingly, he
repaired, and settled at Rouen, giving an early impulsion to
manufactures which has conduced not a little to their great
development since, in the department of the Lower Seine.
After Henry had fallen a victim to domestic treachery, Lee,
envied by the natives whose genius he had eclipsed, was pro-
scribed as a Protestant, and obliged to seek concealment from
the bloody bigots in Paris, where he ended his days in secret
grief and disappointment. Some of his workmen made their
escape into England, where, under his ingenious apprentice,
Aston, they mounted the stocking-frame, with some improvements, and thus restored to its native country an invention
which had been well nigh lost to it.

The first frame was brought into Leicestershire in the year
1640, and thus laid the foundation of the hosiery trade of that
county, since so prodigiously enlarged in it and the adjoining
counties of Nottingham and Derby.

In the year 1663, Charles II. granted to the Framework
Knitters' Society of London, a charter, which had been refused
to them a few years before by Oliver Cromwell.

Jedediah Strutt, the founder of the distinguished house of
Belper, invented, in the year 1758, a machine for making
ribbed stockings. About that time he settled in Derby, and
established that manufacture under the protection of a patent,
in conjunction with his brother-in-law, Mr. Woollatt, a hosier
of that place. During a portion of the patent period, Mr.
Samuel Need, of Nottingham, was a partner in the concern.
The patent right was twice tried in Westminster Hall; first by
the hosiers of Derby, and next by those of Nottingham; after

which it was quietly enjoyed by the patentee till the end of the term of fourteen years. This improvement suggested several more, such as open-work mittens, and fancy articles in the stocking stitch. Andrew Ure. *The Cotton Manufacture of Great Britain*, 1836, II, 338–41

William Felkin (1796–1874), a Nottingham man, entered the stocking trade in 1808 and the lace industry in 1819. He became the local agent for John Heathcoat, the great lace entrepreneur, retiring in 1864 to write his celebrated history of the hosiery and lace manufactures. In the following extract he writes of the state of British industry generally on the eve of the Industrial Revolution.

12 The manufactures of this country were still carried on in the middle of the last century at the homes of the work people usually, and in general on a very limited scale. Though the mercantile marine of England had been gradually extending its visits to distant shores from the time of Elizabeth, and returning with supplies of the products of foreign fields and looms and mines, yet in the main the demand for them was found amongst the upper and middle ranks of society. Very small stocks of wrought articles were kept any where except in cities and towns of note. The bulk of society relied for the supply of necessaries and even of things convenient upon the labour of their own hands in their various crafts, and so getting what they needed by interchange with their neighbours. Travelling even in the busiest parts of England was still slow, along difficult roads, and often not safe ones; therefore internal commerce was as yet advanced but little beyond its infancy.

Whether from the political freedom and security enjoyed during the previous half-century, which always stimulate where they are present the industry of those who by their benign influence enjoy a larger proportion of the results of their labours; or whether from the greater expansion of mind and the direction of its powers to useful purposes amongst the middle classes, arising from the study of the literature of the previous century, added to more extended intercourse with the continent of Europe, there was an undoubted movement upwards in society. Many most important changes were about to be introduced and discoveries and inventions made known, which however accidental some might seem, and none of them perhaps directly traceable to any general cause, yet could not but have resulted from vigorous thought and well conceived design—themselves the symptoms of an improving age.

. . . The local development of inventive skill had some relation, there can be little doubt, to the spirit of enterprize rising into activity all around. Here as elsewhere it was without pretension in the beginning, but very marvellous and unlooked for in its results. The alterations and new constructions in hosiery and lace machinery had become before 1815 so numerous and intricate that Blackner, in his *History*, altogether declined the description of the then later important ones. Fifteen years after, Henson expressed his sense of the difficulty there is in giving numerous mechanical details. . . . Since his publication the duty has become doubly onerous.   William Felkin. *A History of the Machine-Wrought Hosiery and Lace Manufactures*, 1867, 84–6

The Silk Industry   The British silk industry was an old one, long protected by the mercantilist state. It was, however, technically behind its European competitors; Vittorio Zonca's *Novo Teatro di Machine e Edificii* had revealed Italian plans for water-powered silk throwing as early as 1607. The new techniques were monopolised by the Kingdom of Sardinia, and although the arrival in Britain of persecuted French Protestants (including Augustin Courtauld) in the late seventeenth century extended the industry, it was not until 1718 that Sir Thomas Lombe (1685–1739) patented winding, spinning and twisting machinery furtively copied in Italy by his half-brother John (c 1693–1722). Lombe built a large throwing-mill, employing some 300 workers, at Derby in 1721, thus providing a model for subsequent factory development. His patent ended in 1732, when Parliament voted him £14,000 in return for making his machines openly available.

---

13 In the year 1685, the revocation of the edict of Nantes compelled many merchants, manufacturers, and artificers to fly from France. The numbers of these emigrants have been variously stated by different writers, at from 300,000 to 1,000,000 persons. About 70,000 made their way to England and Ireland, with such property as the emergency of their case allowed them to carry away. A large number of them, who had been engaged in the fabrication of silks, resorted to Spitalfields, contributing much, by their knowledge and skill, to the improvement of the manufacture in England. The silks called alamodes and lustrings were introduced by them; and we are also indebted to them for our manufactures in brocades, satins, black and coloured mantuas, black paduasoys, ducapes, watered tabbies, and black velvets, all of which fabrics had previously been imported.

Descendants of many of these refugees still are found in the same spot, engaged in the same occupation. . . .

The manufacture of lustrings and alamode silks, then articles in general use, which, previously to the settlement of the French refugees in Spitalfields, had been imported from France, was, in the year 1692, brought to a state of considerable perfection; the persons engaged therein were this year incorporated by charter, under the name of "the royal lustring company", and obtained from parliament an act, prohibiting the importation of foreign lustrings and alamodes, alleging as the ground for such a restriction in their favour, that which, had it been well founded, should have made them indifferent to all legislative interference—that the manufacture of these articles in England had now reached a greater degree of perfection than was attained by foreigners. . . .

. . . Up to the year 1718, our machinery . . . was so defective, that this country was, in a great degree, dependent upon the throwsters of Italy for the supply of organzined silk; but at that time Mr. Lombe of Derby, having, in the disguise of a common workman, succeeded in taking accurate drawings of silk-throwing machinery in Piedmont, erected a stupendous mill for that purpose on the river Derwent at Derby, and obtained a patent for the sole and exclusive property in the same during the space of fourteen years. This grand machine was constructed with 26,586 wheels, and 97,746 movements, which worked 73,726 yards of organzine silk thread with every revolution of the water wheel whereby the machinery was actuated; and as this revolved three times in each minute, the almost inconceivable quantity of 318,504,960 yards of organzine could be produced daily. Only one water wheel was employed to give motion to the whole of this machinery, the contrivance of which, considering the then state of mechanical science in England, speaks highly for that of the constructor, who possessed the means of controlling and stopping any one or more of the movements at pleasure without obstructing the continued action of the rest. The building wherein this machinery was erected was of great extent, being five stories in height, and occupying one eighth of a mile in length. So long a time was occupied in the construction of this machinery, and so vast was the outlay it occasioned, that the original duration of the patent proved insufficient for the adequate reumeration of its enterprising founder, who, on these grounds, applied to parliament, in the year 1731, for an extension of the term for which his privilege had been granted. This, however, in consideration of the great national importance of the object, which was opposed to its continued limitation in the hands of any individual, was not granted; but parliament voted the sum of 14,000 pounds to sir Thomas Lombe, as some consideration for eminent services rendered by him to the nation, in discovering and introducing, with so much personal risk and labour, and in bringing to perfection at great expense, a work so beneficial to this kingdom; the grant being made upon the sole condition that competent persons should be allowed to execute an exact model of the machinery, to be deposited in such place as his majesty should appoint, in order to diffuse and perpetuate the manufacture. The act authorising the issue of this money mentions, among other causes which justified the grant, the great obstruction offered to sir Thomas Lombe's undertaking by the king of Sardinia, in prohibiting the exportation of the raw silk which the engines were intended to work. Dionysius Lardner (ed). *A Treatise on the Origin, Progressive Improvement, and Present State of the Silk Manufacture*, 1831, 59–60, 63–5 _____

The Linen Industry Linen manufacture was an ancient industry, which was widely established in England, Scotland and Ireland before the Industrial Revolution. In Ulster the industry was encouraged by many landowners and in Scotland by the British Linen Company of 1746 under Lord Justice-Clerk Milton, who was also a trustee of the Scottish Board for improving Fisheries and Manufactures. The company greatly improved on the record of earlier Scottish flax ventures, but gradually declined industrially and became a purely banking concern in 1764. A. J. Warden, a Dundee merchant, here describes the Board's work before it lost its powers in 1823.

_____

14 A Board of Manufactures for Scotland, similar to that for Ireland, was established in the year 1727. There was this difference, however, between the two, that whereas the one was given . . . partly to appease the selfish jealousy of the English nation, and partly to gratify the sectarian ambition of the northern Irish; the other was granted in fulfilment of a fair and open compact between two independent nations, and in satisfaction of what was then generally thought to be the just rights of one of the contracting parties. Both were undoubtedly economical blunders, but only one can be said to have been a political crime. By the Treaty of Union between England and Scotland (signed 22d July, 1706), it was stipulated that certain annuities should be paid out of the imperial purse, and applied specially for the benefit of the latter country, as equivalent for the greater advantages which, it was supposed, would accrue to the former by that treaty. The establishment of the Scottish Board of Manufactures was the tardy carrying out of that stipulation.

In the act or order in Council appointing the Board, and which was entituled "His Majesty's patent for improving Fisheries and Manufactures in Scotland", we accordingly find the preamble running thus:—"Considering that, by the 15th Act of the Treaty of Union, it is provided that an annuity of £2000 per annum be appropriated for seven years for promoting manufactures of Coarse Wool: Considering that, by Act 5th Geo. I., an annuity of £2000 per annum be payable out of the revenues of Scotland in lieu of the equivalent claimed by Scotland under the Treaty of Union, to be applied to the encouragement of the Fisheries and Manufactures of Scotland," and so on.

. . . I have not been able to learn when the spinning wheel was first introduced into Scotland, but it is clear, from the establishment of the Spinning Schools by the Board in 1727, that it was little known, or at least, little used, at that period in many districts of the country. And we do know that the good old fashioned rock and spindle had not been wholly superseded even so late as the beginning of the present century. . . . The wheels of 1727 were single-handed, for the double-handed wheel was not invented till about the year 1764. It is spoken of as "A great improvement in the spinning-wheel, whereby a child can spin twice as much as a grown person can do with the common wheel".

At the date of the establishment of the Board, the returns of Linen stamped in the different counties shew that the manufacture was pretty generally prevalent over the whole of Scotland. Its chief localities, however, were in those counties lying in the great valley which extends from Lanarkshire in the west to Forfarshire in the east,—our own county (Forfarshire) being even then far ahead of all the others. Out of 2,183,000 yards stamped in Scotland in 1727, Forfarshire had 596,000; Perthshire, 477,000; Fifeshire, 362,000; and Lanarkshire, 272,000.

Soon after this the manufacture began gradually to creep east-
ward, especially after the introduction of the cotton manufacture into the western counties about the end of last century; the
testimony of the Board being that wherever the manufacture of
cotton was established, that of Linen sensibly declined; until, in
1822, the last year in which the returns were made, out of
36,268,000 yards . . . Forfarshire had 22,629,000 yards; Fifeshire, 7,923,000; Perthshire, 1,605,000; and Lanarkshire, 22,869.
All the other counties, with the exception of Aberdeenshire,
which had 2,500,000 yards, having only a few thousand yards
each, and in some the manufacture had entirely disappeared.

. . . The first mill for the spinning of yarn by machinery was
erected in Brigton near Glammis, in 1790, by Messrs. James
Ivory and Co., relatives, I believe of the present Lord Ivory. . . .
Alexander J. Warden. *The Linen Trade, Ancient and Modern,*
1864, 233–4, 237–9

The Weaver The aristocrat of the domestic textile industries
was, almost inevitably, the weaver. Independent, comparatively prosperous and through the eighteenth century seem-
ingly secure from the new machinery which revolutionised
spinning and consequently enhanced the handloom-weaver's
status and income, the weaver was widely admired. The
weaving fraternities themselves included a surprising number
of writers, such as William Thom (1789–1848), the 'Bard of
Inverury', and Joshua Hobson (1811–76), the Huddersfield
Chartist and Conservative journalist. And contemporary observers regularly commended the weavers, particularly in
retrospect after the Napoleonic wars, when the hand-weavers'
easily acquired craft attracted cheap Irish labour and simultaneously faced ever-increasing competition from the power-
looms. A Paisley writer regarded the weavers as 'the most
numerous, the most industrious, and, perhaps, the most
virtuous of your manufacturing operatives', in 1826. In the
following extract an anonymous divine advises a still-growing
and increasingly important late eighteenth-century group.

15 Once more, methinks I cannot but observe, how the wisdom of divine providence hath made work for all the children of men, that as there was no beggar in Israel, so there need be no beggars in England. How many doth a single weaver imploy of all, both sexes and sizes! It must be an adult man must weave, but women must spin for him, and children must fill his pipes. It is the reproach of England that there are so many beggars in the streets thereof; when God hath furnished it with one little beast, whose profit, if improved, would set them all to work and afford them bread in the sweat of their face. That we are full of scandalous beggars, is not because the providence of God hath not laid out work enough, or the trading of England is so little, that it will not set them to it; nor because the legislative power hath not provided sufficient laws; but because they are so ill executed by inferiour officers, and parents are suffered to bring up children in idleness. O England! Spit out thy flegm, shake off thy sloth, honour God in the substance and increase which he hath given thee. It is nothing but lust and sloth that fills thee with such prodigious wickedness and beggary.

 . . . A second advantage of this trade is the little time that it giveth either servant or master (but servants especially) for idleness. Idleness (especially in youth) is the source and fountain of almost all the debauchery that polluteth the world, and all the beggary with which we abound. . . .

 . . . It is the idle person that proves the gamester, the drunkard, etc. It is true there may be an excess of labour, when it is to that degree that it wasteth the body, destroyeth the health, allows not due time for devotion, nor the reasonable repairs of the body, by food or sleep, or moderate recreation; but (these things excepted) the lesser time for idleness any trade allows, the better it is. This I am sure this trade doth. I am many many times ashamed of my own bed, when I see the candles in the poor Weavers chambers or hear the noise of their looms.

Thirdly, It is the advantage of this above many other trades, that a man may be dealing in it with a little stock, and from it get a little livelihood. It is the disadvantage of many other employments, that nothing can be done in them without several hundreds of pounds going: 'tis otherwise in this, my self have known many who came to considerable estates, who have told me they begun with ten pound; they passed but with a staff over Jordan, and at their coming back had great droves.

Fourthly, If God blasts the Weaver in his course of trade, yet (provided he hath his health and limbs) his trade affords him a livelihood. Many trades do not this, they are more open, &c. And if the tradesman fails, he is forced to fly.

Fifthly, If God blesseth the Weaver in his trade, he is fitted by it also in a great measure for the more noble employment of a merchant: he hath learned to know the true making and the prices of most stuffs, how they may be afforded, &c.

Sixthly, It gives a great advantage for some exercises of religion to be interwoven with secular employment. It is the great unhappiness of some employments, that they do so wholly take up the head and heart of such as are engaged in them, that they hardly allow any intervals for any spiritual employment. The Weaver is not so; but his trade is very consistent with, 1. heavenly ejaculation; . . . he may weave and pray. 2. spiritual meditations . . . 3. spiritual discourse. Ordinarily three or four are working here together in the same chamber: if but one of them will be the preacher, the others are tyed to be the hearers; and indeed I have often thought (how truly I cannot tell) that this trade this way hath very much contributed to the religion of this town, God having a great number of that occupation among us, of whom we have reason to hope very well, as to their eternal state.

Seventhly, It is a trade of great ingenuity: no mechanick trade (if this may be called so) giving such an advantage to ingenious persons to improve their fancy, by the invention of new patterns, or mixing yarns and colours too for a new pattern laid before them.

Lastly, it is a trade infinitely useful as to the poor. Females both women and children are imployed in preparing their yarn: children from their infancy almost, in winding their pipes, men in weaving at the loom. In short, I cannot tell whether there be any one other employment, that affords so many personal advantages to the tradesman, or political advantages to the state under whose government they are employed. . . .

This observation may be of a double use to the Weaver. 1. To restrain his discontent for the course of life, in which the providence of God, the prudence of his parents or governors, and his own choice in his younger years, have engaged him. It is a great infirmity of our natures, that not one of many is content with his portion . . . but what hath the Weaver to complain of? What can commend a trade which is wanting to his? The Alehouse-keeper, Vintner, Inn-keeper, may lie down many a night with an aking heart, to think how many he hath been helping on to the bottomless pit. Others may have sour reflections, when they come home at night to think over what they have been doing that day, and their consciences make them answer, that they have been serving the world with what is of no use, but to serve pride or luxury. The weaver's conscience shall never trouble him for this. When the weaver reflects upon his trade, and considers the general end of it approved by God, the profit of it, tho' not so great as others, yet what will afford food and raiment to the industrious hand, the advantages of it, whether God pleaseth in it to smile or frown upon him, the advantage it gives him for devout ejaculations, pious meditations, good conferences, the usefulness of it for all, more especially for the maintenance of the poor, he hath no reason to murmur at divine providence, nor to blame his parents' prudence, or reflect upon his youthful indiscretion. God hath chosen a good lot for him, and he ought cheerfully to abide in the calling to which God hath called him, and to be content.

2. Did I say to be content? Yea to be highly thankful unto God, blessing God that by his providence directed him to such an employ in the world, as his conscience shall never justly

check him for the following of it; such a one as he can in faith go to God morning and evening, and beg God's blessing upon, so cannot many a jollier person. An employment in which he hath many advantages, more than in many others, to serve his God, himself, his generation; that he shall not live in the earth like a drone, upon the honey gathered by others, nor like a beast of prey upon rapine, nor like one who thinks he is only born for himself, and whom, both the good and sober world, could a thousand times with less inconvenience miss than keep alive. Here is abundance of matter of praise, that hath over-ruled our wills in the indiscretion of our youth to such a choice as this, the choice of a trade at which a man may sit with so much satisfaction, and in which he may work with so much pleasure, and the exercise of so much piety, and for so much publick profit, as well as private advantage. Let then the weaver, reflecting on his employment, sit and sing.

. . . For the most part, those who begin with the least stock, raise the best estates.

It is an observation which will be found to justify itself, as in many other trades and courses of life, so in this trade also. Not many who begin with large stocks, grow rich by trading; but for the most part, the most thriving part of tradesmen are those who begin with little; nor doth the reason of this ly wholly out of ordinary sight, though possibly something of it may not be so obvious.

. . . Lastly, I observe, That hardly any trades will maintain their glory, without some government; every particular trades-man having neither wit nor honesty enough to be a law to himself. In all considerable trades therefore, prudent statesmen thought fit to make corporations, where the multitude are under the inspection, rule and government of the most ex-perienced, wise and discreet men of that occupation. And most trades, which to any considerable degree multiply tradesmen, either have such governours, or in a short time come to nothing for want of them.

. . . To this purpose, ordinarily such tradesmen are left to chuse their own governours, as being best acquainted with the trade, and the persons that have most skill in it, and have best approved their honesty in the managery of it. J.C., *D.D.* *The Weaver's Pocket-Book: or Weaving Spiritualized. In a Discourse, Wherein Men employed in that Occupation, are instructed how to raise Heavenly Meditations, from the several Parts of their Work. To which also are added Some few Moral and Spiritual Observations, relating both to That and other Trades,* Dundee, 1766, 92–3, 147–57, 159, 218, 224

———

Frederick Engels (1820–95), the friend of and collaborator with Karl Marx (1818–83), was the son of a prosperous textile manufacturer in the Wuppertal district of the Rhineland. He was sent to his father's Manchester firm in 1843 and at once started the research for his classic description of working-class life in 1844. The co-founder of modern Communism was a rather strange man, combining foxhunting with management of an anti-reform firm, the subsidising of Marx, doting over his mistress and condemning bourgeois 'immorality'. He published his account of English working-class conditions in German at Leipzig in 1845. Many details were incorrect, particularly when the work was translated into English for the New York and London editions of 1887 and 1892. The following extract, however, does not depend upon any mis-transcription or mis-translation of documents. Here Engels paints an idealised picture of the weaver and incidentally reveals his own political and moral attitudes. His views were based on a brief experience of English industry; but they are still reprinted in Moscow.

———

16 The history of the proletariat in England begins with the second half of the last century, with the invention of the steam-engine and of machinery for working cotton. These inventions gave rise, as is well known, to an industrial revolution, a revolution which altered the whole civil society; one, the historical importance of which is only now beginning to be recognised. England is the classic soil of this transformation, which was all the mightier, the more silently it proceeded; and England is, therefore, the classic land of its chief product also, the proletariat. Only in England can the proletariat be studied in all its relations and from all sides.

We have not, here and now, to deal with the history of this revolution, nor with its vast importance for the present and the future. Such a delineation must be reserved for a future, more comprehensive work. For the moment, we must limit ourselves to the little that is necessary for understanding the facts that follow, for comprehending the present state of the English proletariat.

Before the introduction of machinery, the spinning and weaving of raw materials was carried on in the working-man's home. Wife and daughter spun the yarn that the father wove or that they sold, if he did not work it up himself. These weaver families lived in the country in the neighbourhood of the towns, and could get on fairly well with their wages, because the home market was almost the only one, and the crushing power of competition that came later, with the conquest of foreign markets and the extension of trade, did not yet press upon wages. There was, further, a constant increase in the demand for the home market, keeping pace with the slow increase in population and employing all the workers; and there was also the impossibility of vigorous competition of the workers among themselves, consequent upon the rural dispersion of their homes. So it was that the weaver was usually in a position to lay by something, and rent a little piece of land, that he cultivated in his leisure hours, of which he had as many as he chose to take, since he could weave whenever and as long as he pleased. True, he was a bad farmer and managed his land inefficiently, often obtaining but poor crops; nevertheless, he was no proletarian, he had a stake in the country, he was permanently settled, and stood one step higher in society than the English workman of to-day.

So the workers vegetated throughout a passably comfortable existence, leading a righteous and peaceful life in all piety and

E

probity; and their material position was far better than that
of their successors. They did not need to over-work; they did
no more than they chose to do, and yet earned what they
needed. They had leisure for healthful work in garden or field,
work which, in itself, was recreation for them, and they could
take part besides in the recreations and games of their neighbours, and all these games—bowling, cricket, football, etc.,
contributed to their physical health and vigour. They were,
for the most part, strong, well-built people, in whose physique
little or no difference from that of their peasant neighbours was
discoverable. Their children grew up in the fresh country air,
and, if they could help their parents at work, it was only
occasionally; while of eight or twelve hours work for them
there was no question.

What the moral and intellectual character of this class was
may be guessed. Shut off from the towns, which they never
entered, their yarn and woven stuff being delivered to travelling agents for payment of wages—so shut off that old people
who lived quite in the neighbourhood of the town never went
thither until they were robbed of their trade by the introduction
of machinery and obliged to look about them in the towns for
work—the weavers stood upon the moral and intellectual plane
of the yeomen with whom they were usually immediately connected through their little holdings. They regarded their
squire, the greatest landholder of the region, as their natural
superior; they asked advice of him, laid their small disputes
before him for settlement, and gave him all honour, as this
patriarchal relation involved. They were "respectable" people,
good husbands and fathers, led moral lives because they had no
temptation to be immoral, there being no groggeries or low
houses in their vicinity, and because the host, at whose inn they
now and then quenched their thirst was also a respectable man,
usually a large tenant farmer who took pride in his good order,
good beer, and early hours. They had their children the whole
day at home, and brought them up in obedience and the fear of
God; the patriarchal relationship remained undisturbed so

long as the children were unmarried. The young people grew up in idyllic simplicity and intimacy with their playmates until they married; and even though sexual intercourse before marriage almost unfailingly took place, this happened only when the moral obligation of marriage was recognised on both sides, and a subsequent wedding made everything good. In short, the English industrial workers of those days lived and thought after the fashion still to be found here and there in Germany, in retirement and seclusion, without mental activity and without violent fluctuations in their position in life. They could rarely read and far more rarely write; went regularly to church, never talked politics, never conspired, never thought, delighted in physical exercises, listened with inherited reverence when the Bible was read, and were, in their unquestioning humility, exceedingly well-disposed towards the 'superior' classes. But intellectually, they were dead; lived only for their petty, private interest, for their looms and gardens, and knew nothing of the mighty movement which, beyond their horizon, was sweeping through mankind. They were comfortable in their silent vegetation, and but for the industrial revolution they would never have emerged from this existence, which, cosily romantic as it was, was nevertheless not worthy of human beings. In truth, they were not human beings; they were merely toiling machines in the service of the few aristocrats who had guided history down to that time. The industrial revolution has simply carried this out to its logical end by making the workers machines pure and simple, taking from them the last trace of independent activity, and so forcing them to think and demand a position worthy of men. As in France politics, so in England manufacture, and the movement of civil society in general drew into the whirl of history the last classes which had remained sunk in apathetic indifference to the universal interests of mankind.

The first invention which gave rise to a radical change in the state of the English workers was the jenny, invented in the year 1764 by a weaver, James Hargreaves, of Standhill, near Blackburn, in North Lancashire. This machine was the rough beginning of the later invented mule, and was moved by hand. Instead of one spindle like the ordinary spinning-wheel, it carried sixteen or eighteen manipulated by a single workman. This invention made it possible to deliver more yarn than heretofore. Whereas, though one weaver had employed three spinners, there had never been enough yarn, and the weaver had often been obliged to wait for it, there was now more yarn to be had than could be woven by the available workers. The demand for woven goods, already increasing, rose yet more in consequence of the cheapness of these goods, which cheapness, in turn, was the outcome of the diminished cost of producing the yarn. More weavers were needed, and weavers' wages rose. Now that the weaver could earn more at his loom, he gradually abandoned his farming, and gave his whole time to weaving. At that time a family of four grown persons and two children (who were set to spooling) could earn, with ten hours' daily work, four pounds sterling in a week, and often more if trade was good and work pressed. It happened often enough that a single weaver earned two pounds a week at his loom. By degrees the class of farming weavers wholly disappeared, and was merged in the newly arising class of weavers who lived wholly upon wages, had no property whatever, not even the pretended property of a holding, and so became working-men, proletarians. Moreover, the old relation between spinner and weaver was destroyed. Hitherto, so far as this had been possible, yarn had been spun and woven under one roof. Now that the jenny as well as the loom required a strong hand, men began to spin, and whole families lived by spinning, while others laid the antiquated, superseded spinning-wheel aside; and, if they had not means of purchasing a jenny, were forced to live upon the wages of the father alone. Thus began with spinning and weaving that division of labour which has since been so infinitely perfected. Frederick Engels. *The Condition of the Working-Class in England in 1844*, English edn, 1892, trans Mrs F. K. Wischnewetzky, 1–5

Samuel Bamford (1788–1872), a prominent Lancashire Radical in the early nineteenth century, was brought up at Middleton, among weaving folk. His education was varied but largely rested on the local Sunday school. In two autobiographical books Bamford looked back over both a long political career and a long industrial experience. In the following extract he describes the actual life of a handloom weaver in the late eighteenth-century 'golden age'. A weaver himself, he wrote from personal experience of working-class life and politics.

---

17 My parents were a worthy and honest couple, residing, when I was born, in the town of Middleton, near Manchester. My father was a weaver of muslin, at that time considered a fine course of work, and requiring a superior hand; whilst my mother found plenty of employment in occasional weaving, in winding bobbins, or pins for my father, and in looking after the house and the children, of whom I was the fourth born, and the third then living. I have always been given to understand that I was brought into the world on the 28th of February, in "the Gallic eara—eighty-eight"; when, certainly, many of the world's troubles, as well as my own, had a beginning. My parents were religious, of which further shall appear hereafter. My father, for his station in life, was a superior man. He had many talents both natural and acquired, which in those days were not often possessed by men of his condition in society. He was considerably imbued with book knowledge, particularly of a religious kind; wrote a good hand; understood arithmetic; had some acquaintance with astronomy; was a vocal and instrumental musician, singing from the book and playing on the flute; he had a deep taste for melody, as I can recollect from the tunes he played; he was likewise an occasional composer of music, and introduced several of his pieces amongst the religious body with which he was connected; he was also a writer of verses, of no mean order, as I shall presently shew,—so that, take him for all in all, he stood far above his rustic acquaintance in the village, and had to endure the usual consequences

—envy, and detraction from the meanest of them. During the hot blood of his youth, few young men could stand before him, either in the wrestling bout, or the battle. I have heard it told, that in those days, notwithstanding his taste for books, and music, and other means for true enjoyment, he at times, associated with the wild rough fellows of the neighbourhood, at the Church Ale-house, or at the Boar's Head Inn; and drank, danced, or, when nothing less would do, fought with the moodiest or merriest of them. . . .

But irregularities like these, of my father's young days, violent probably in proportion to their unfrequency, could not be indulged in without producing their natural consequences. His health was impaired; he took cold after cold, and disregarded them; and at length a violent fever laid him prostrate at the verge of the grave. On his recovery he was an altered man. His own natural sense, supported by the serious advice of relatives and friends, determined him on endeavouring to lead a different life. Being convinced that the course he had pursued was fraught with evil as well as folly, he sought divine aid in abandoning it, and he joined a society of Methodists, of which his parents and several individuals of the family were already members.

When his health had become re-established, neither his good resolutions nor God's help forsook him. He continued a member of the religious society he had joined; became "a burning and a shining light," as the Methodists term an exemplary young member; and soon afterwards marrying my mother, he set forward, as we may say, on his pilgrimage through this world, and "Zion-ward". In due time a young family began to sprout about his heels, and with a view to meet increasing expenditure, he and a brother of his named Thomas, adventured a small capital of money in the spinning line, which was then done by jenny; and in weaving their yarns into grey cloths. They succeeded in proportion to their most sanguine expectations, for there was then a market for anything which the spindle or the hand-loom could make,—and they were about to realize all

they had dared to hope, when a member of their religious body
—one of their "brethren in Israel"—piqued as they supposed,
by their increasing influence in a religious, as well as worldly
sense, suddenly called on them for the repayment of a sum
which he had lent them for the purpose of commencing their
business, and persisting in his demand, they sold off their stock
of cloth and machinery, paid every farthing they owed, and
closed their concern, my father sitting down to the business of
schoolmaster, and my uncle resuming the manual operations
of a weaver and small farmer. Difficulties still increased with
the wants of our family; my father's school profits were not
sufficiently steady to be depended upon, and he relinquished
them and returned to the loom. The throes of the French
Revolution, and the excitement they created in England, soon
afterwards deranged both money transactions and mercantile
affairs. Banks stopped, payments were suspended, and trade
was at a stand. Woe to the poor weaver then, with his loom
without work, the provision shop without credit, and his wife
and weans foodless, and looking at each other, and at him, as
if saying—Husband! father! hast thou neither bread nor hope
for us?

 . . . It would be about a hundred and thirty-two years since,
or the year 1716, that my father's grandfather, James Bamford,
lived in Hools Wood, in Thornham, keeping there a small farm,
and making cane reeds for weavers of flannel and course
cotton. Of his children I know not anything, save that he had
many sons from whom the Bamfords of Middleton, Alkrington,
Tonge, and some other neighbouring places are descended.
According to what was handed down in our branch of his
posterity, he was the next heir to the estate of Bamford Hall . . .
[but] the rightful heirs [were] cut off from the property, which
had descended through the ancestors from the time when the
Saxon wrested it from the Celt.

My grandfather was Daniel Bamford, the youngest son of
this James Bamford. He came to reside at Middleton, and was
a small farmer and weaver. He married Hannah, the daughter

of Samuel Cheetham, who was a watch and clock maker, and was, consequently, considered something better in condition than common in those days. . . . My grandfather and all his family had been strict church goers, but on their joining the Methodists, their attendance at church was less constant than it had been. . . .

My great grandfather, Samuel Cheetham, was a thorough "King's-man". During the troubles in 1745, he loaded his gun, and swore he would blow out the brains of any rebel who interfered with him; and judging from his conduct on several occasions, there is but small reason for supposing he would not have been as good as his word. . . .

. . . My mother's father, Jeffrey Battersby, who was quite his opposite in person, manner, and sentiment, was with the Pretender's party at the Boar's Head, assisting them in the collection of King's taxes, and in the levying of contributions; in which his local knowledge, and his quick perception, would, doubtless, be very useful. . . .

As I was getting rather too unmanageable for my aunt at the bobbin-wheel, fortunately in this respect, for both her and myself, my brother went to reside at Manchester, and a vacancy thus occurring on one of the looms, I was transferred to it, and became a weaver. . . .

Having now become an active lad, and, from my good temper and willingness to perform any service, now that the abhorent wheel was not in the way, had made some advances into the kindly feelings of my aunt and uncle, I was at times chosen to assist the latter when he took the work home to Manchester. The family were, at that time, chiefly employed by Messrs. Samuel and James Broadbent, of Cannon-street, and as the work was for the most part "pollicat" and "romoll" hand-kerchiefs, with a finer reed, occasionally, of silk and cotton "gar-ments", or handkerchiefs, the "bearing home wallet" was often both bulky and heavy; and when it happened to be too much so for one person to carry, a neighbour's wallet would be borrowed, the burden divided into two, and I would go with one part over my shoulder, behind or before my uncle. He being, as already stated, rather heavy in person would walk deliberately, with a stick in his hand, his green woollen apron twisted round his waist, his clean shirt showing at the open breast of his waist-coat, his brown silk handkerchief wrapped round his neck, a quid of tobacco in his mouth, and a broad and rather slouched hat on his head. So would he appear when setting out on a "bearing home" journey; whilst I, with my smaller wallet, with my rough jacket, my knee breeches, my strong stockings and shoes, my open collared shirt, and pleasure and glee in my heart and countenance, footed the way as lightsomely as a young colt. Our road then lay up the brow at Alkrington, which was a pleasant foot-path through fields,—past Nut Bank, or the Tan-pits, whichever we chose,—along Hill-lane, through the village of Blakeley, over Tetlow Bridge, across Smedley Fields, over the Butter Stile, and along the highroad, and down Red Bank, into Manchester.

The warehouse of Messrs. Broadbent was nearly at the top of Cannon-street, on the right hand side. We mounted some steps, went along a covered passage, and up a height or two of stairs, to a landing place, one side of which was railed off by the bannister, and the other furnished with a seat for weavers to rest upon when they arrived. Here we should probably find some half dozen weavers and winders, waiting for their turn to deliver in their work and to receive fresh material; and the business betwixt workman and putter-out was generally done in an amicable, reasonable way. No captious fault-finding, no bullying, no arbitrary abatement, which have been too common since, were then practiced. If the work were really faulty, the weaver was shewn the fault; and if it were not a serious one he was only cautioned against repeating it; if the length or the weight was not what it should be, he was told of it, and would be expected to set it right, or account for it, at his next bearing home, and if he were a frequent defaulter he was no longer employed. But very rarely indeed did it happen that any tran-saction bearing the appearance of an advantage being taken against the workman by the putter out was heard of in those days.

It would sometimes happen that warp or weft would not be ready until after dinner, and on such occasions, my uncle having left his wallet in the care of the putter-out, would go down stairs and get paid at the counting-house, and from thence go to the public house where we lunched on bread and cheese, or cold meat and bread, with ale, to which my uncle added his ever-favourite pipe of tobacco. This house, which was The Hope and Anchor, in the Old Church yard, was also frequented by other weavers; the putter-out at Broadbent's generally dined there in the parlour, and when he had dined he would come and take a glass of ale, smoke his pipe, and chat with the weavers, after which, my uncle would again go to the warehouse, and getting what material he wanted, would buy a few groceries and tobacco in the town, or probably, as we returned through the apple market, to go down Long Mill Gate, he would purchase a peck of apples, and giving them to me to carry, we wended towards home, I, by permission, making pretty free with the apples by the way. Before leaving the town my uncle would probably call at the Queen Anne, in Long Mill Gate, to see if there were any suitable company going our way; if there were, we took a glass until all were ready, and then we walked on together. Another calling house was Schofield's, at Scotland Bridge, and the last in the town was The Flower Pot, on Red Bank. In winter time, and especially when day was closing, the weavers preferred thus returning in groups, for the road was not altogether free of foot-pads any more than at present. In hot summer weather, the weavers would sometimes indulge themselves by a ride in a cart, or they would leave their heavy burdens at The Three Crowns, in Cock Gates, to be forwarded by Abraham Lees, the Middleton carrier. When a party of weavers returned in company, they would generally make a halt at Blakeley, either at The White Lion, or at Travis's, The Golden Lion, over the way. There the wallets, or "pokes" as they were mostly called, were piled in a heap, ale was ordered, seats drawn round the fire, pipes were soon lighted, news interchanged with the host or some of his company; half an hour, or sometimes more, was thus spent, when the shot being called and paid, the travellers took their wallets and climbing the Hill-lane, were soon at home. Such was "a bearing home day" to Manchester in those times.

But even those days, advantageous as they certainly were when compared with the present ones which are devoted to a similar errand, were considered as being greatly altered for the worse since the days which could be spoken of from remembrance. The two classes of workman and employer were already at too great a distance from each other, and it was a subject of observation that the masters were becoming more and more proud and uplifted each day. Some had seen the time when, on taking their work home, and material not being ready, a dialogue like the following would take place.

Master.—Well, William, there will be no piece for thee till afternoon.

Weaver.—Very well, I'll wait for it then: wot time munni come, think'n yo?

Master.—Why, it's nearly dinner time now, and if thou'll go an' have a bit o' dinner wi' me, th' work will, mayhap, be ready when we come back.

Weaver.—Thank yo, mester, I'll goo wi' yo then.

So master and man would walk together to some decent looking house, in some decent, quiet street, where the master, his wife, his children, and the guest, would sit down to a plain substantial dinner of broth most likely, with dumpling and meat, or roast beef and baked pudding, or a steaming potatoe pie; after which, master and workman would sit with their ale and pipes, talking about whatever most concerned themselves. . . . Samuel Bamford. *Early Days*, 1849, 1–5, 11–13, 15, 18, 115–20

The Entrepreneurs and Inventors

The Industrial Revolution in the textile industries developed from a variety of causes. The comparative freedom of British society, Britain's internal free trade, the decay and weak enforcement of State restraints and controls, the 'Agricultural Revolution', the population rise, the development of transport and banking services, and the availability of cheap capital all played a part. Dissenting schools in England, catering for middle-class groups largely precluded from political, military, and 'official' careers, and the Presbyterian system of education in Scotland taught new disciplines and new codes. An interest in research, discovery, invention, and application of new techniques was fostered: the Society of Arts and Parliament would periodically reward inventors; provincial societies, notably the Lunar Society of Birmingham, further encouraged scientific discussion; and an atmosphere was created in which the inventor and the exploiter of the invention were regarded as benefactors of society—except, of course, by those whose occupations were affected. Anglican-dominated Oxford, Cambridge, and grammar schools (despite Leeds Grammar School's famous legal defeat when attempting to extend its curriculum) probably played a larger part than some historians have allowed: a connection between the 'Protestant Ethic' and the 'Rise of Capitalism' has had a long popularity. Certainly, late eighteenth-century interest in 'inventions' was widespread: James Watt

76

worked on his steam engines as an employee of Professor Joseph Black, of Glasgow University; Lancashire workmen furtively improved early machines; and such aristocrats as the 9th Earl of Dundonald and the 2nd Marquess of Rockingham spent fortunes on experimental work. The role of individual inventors and industrial organisers is controversial and is often minimised for various reasons, not least because their importance was exaggerated by Victorian writers. Nevertheless, the factory system can only be understood after some examination of these men and of the society within which they worked.

The Climate of Opinion   Probably the most influential and certainly the most famous commentator on economic matters in the late eighteenth century was Adam Smith (1723–90). The son of a Scottish civil servant, he was educated at Glasgow and Oxford universities, and subsequently lectured at Edinburgh and Glasgow before touring the Continent with the Duke of Buccleuch. His great inquiry into the *Wealth of Nations* appeared in 1776, after many years' work. It proclaimed the doctrines of individual self-interest and natural liberty as the fundamentals of sensible economics. Although Governments only slowly moved away from mercantilism to *laisser-faire*, Smith's regularly republished work and the popular vulgarisations of it had a seminal effect on national attitudes.

---

18   Every individual is continually exerting himself to find out the most advantageous employment for whatever capital he can command. It is his own advantage, indeed, and not that of the society, which he has in view. But the study of his own advantage naturally, or rather necessarily, leads him to prefer that employment which is most advantageous to the society.

. . . As every individual, therefore, endeavours as much as he can both to employ his capital in the support of domestic industry, and so to direct that industry that its produce may be of the greatest value; every individual necessarily labours to render the annual revenue of the society as great as he can.

He generally, indeed, neither intends to promote the public interest, nor knows how much he is promoting it. By preferring the support of domestic to that of foreign industry, he intends only his own security; and by directing that industry in such a manner as its produce may be of the greatest value, he intends only his own gain, and he is in this, as in many other cases, led by an invisible hand to promote an end which was no part of his intention. Nor is it always the worse for the society that it was no part of it. By pursuing his own interest he frequently promotes that of the society more effectually than when he really intends to promote it. I have never known much good done by those who affected to trade for the public good. It is an affectation, indeed, not very common among merchants, and very few words need be employed in dissuading them from it.

. . . To give the monopoly of the home market to the produce of domestic industry, in any particular art or manufacture, is in some measure to direct private people in what manner they ought to employ their capitals, and must, in almost all cases, be either a useless or a hurtful regulation. If the produce of domestic can be bought there as cheap as that of foreign industry, the regulation is evidently useless. If it cannot, it must generally be hurtful. It is the maxim of every prudent master of a family never to attempt to make at home what it will cost him more to make than to buy. The tailor does not attempt to make his own shoes, but buys them from the shoemaker. The shoemaker does not attempt to make his own clothes, but employs a tailor. The farmer attempts to make neither the one nor the other, but employs those different artificers. All of them find it for their interest to employ their whole industry in a way in which they have some advantage over their neighbours, and to purchase with a part of its produce or what is the same thing, with the price of a part of it, whatever else they have occasion for.

What is prudence in the conduct of every private family can scarce be folly in that of a great kingdom. If a foreign country can supply us with a commodity cheaper than we ourselves can make it, better buy it from them with some part of the produce of our own industry employed in a way in which we have some advantage. The general industry of the country, being always in proportion to the capital which employs it, will not thereby be diminished, no more than that of the above mentioned artificers; but only left to find out the way in which it can be employed with the greatest advantage. It is certainly not employed to the greatest advantage when it is thus directed towards an object which it can buy cheaper than it can make. The value of its annual produce is certainly more or less diminished when it is thus turned away from producing commodities evidently of more value than the commodity which it is directed to produce. . . .

. . . The natural advantages which one country has over another in producing particular commodities are sometimes so great that it is acknowledged by all the world to be vain to struggle with them. By means of glasses, hotbeds, and hot walls, very good grapes can be raised in Scotland, and very good wine too can be made from them at about thirty times the expense for which at least equally good can be brought from foreign countries. Would it be a reasonable law to prohibit the importation of all foreign wines merely to encourage the making of claret and burgundy in Scotland? . . . Adam Smith. *An Inquiry into the Nature and Causes of the Wealth of Nations*, 1776, Book iv, ch 2

————

Patrick Colquhoun (1745–1820), a Glasgow man, was an early collector of statistical information. While working as a stipendiary magistrate in London he developed an interest in local criminal and pauper statistics. In 1814 he produced his major collection of details on the British economy. The following excerpt expresses the new confidence which their recent achievements had given to early nineteenth-century Britons.

————

19 It is impossible to contemplate the progress of manufactures in Great Britain within the last thirty years without wonder and astonishment. Its rapidity, particularly since the commencement of the French revolutionary war, exceeds all credibility. The improvement of the steam engines, but above all the facilities afforded to the great branches of the woollen and cotton manufactories by ingenious machinery, invigorated by capital and skill, are beyond all calculation; and as these machines are rendered applicable to silk, linen, hosiery and various other branches, the increased produce, assisted by human labour, is so extensive that it does more than counter-balance the difference between the price of labour in this, and other countries:—the latter cannot enjoy the same facilities without those extensive capitals, skill, and experience which the British manufacturers have acquired, and which cannot be transferred to foreign nations without those requisites (capital and skill) which they will probably not possess for a long series of years, and which very few of them can ever hope to enjoy. These considerations are sufficient to allay all fears or appre-hensions of any injurious competition in the foreign market, provided the improvements shall continue as heretofore to be progressive. Patrick Colquhoun. *A Treatise on the Wealth, Power, and Resources of the British Empire*, 2nd edn, 1815, 68 _____

Domestic woollen workers in the West Riding for long opposed the extension of the factory system. They had con-siderable support from others—such as Sir James Graham of Kirkstall, who found it 'very pleasing to see domestic Clothiers living in fields . . . rather than shut up in streets'—and exercised a sizeable influence on county politics. In 1806, however, a Committee of the House of Commons shared the optimism of the factory-owners, stressing the advantages derived from the development of factories and machinery. 'The apprehensions entertained of factories', it proclaimed, 'are not only vicious in principle, but . . . practically erroneous; to such a degree, that even the very opposite dispositions might be reasonably enter-tained. . . .' In the following extract from the Committee's Report early nineteenth-century attitudes are expressed in typical fashion.

20 ... The rapid and prodigious increase of late years in the Manufactures and Commerce of this Country is universally known, as well as the effects of that increase on our Revenue and National Strength; and in considering the immediate causes of that Augmentation, it will appear that, under the favour of Providence, it is principally to be ascribed to the general spirit of enterprise and industry among a free and en-lightened People, left to the unrestrained exercise of their talents in the employment of a vast capital; pushing to the utmost the principle of the division of labour; calling in all the resources of scientific research and mechanical ingenuity; and, finally, availing themselves of all the benefits to be derived from visiting Foreign Countries, not only for forming new, and con-firming old commercial connections, but for obtaining a per-sonal knowledge of the wants, the taste, the habits, the dis-coveries and improvements, the productions and fabrics of other civilized Nations, and, by thus bringing home facts and suggestions, perfecting our existing Manufactures, and adding new ones to our domestic stock; opening at the same time new markets for the product of our manufacturing and commercial industry, and qualifying ourselves for supplying them. It is by these means alone, and, above all, your Committee must re-peat it, by the effect of Machinery in improving the quality and cheapening the fabrication of our various Articles of Export, that with a continually accumulating weight of taxes, and with all the necessaries and comforts of life gradually increasing in price, the effects of which on the wages of labour could not but be very considerable, our Commerce and Manufactures have also been increasing in such a degree as to surpass the most sanguine calculations of the ablest political writers who had speculated on the improvements of a future age. ...

... The right of every man to employ the capital he inherits, or has acquired, according to his own discretion, without molestation or obstruction, so long as he does not infringe on the rights or property of others, is one of those privileges which

F

the free and happy Constitution of this Country has long accustomed every Briton to consider as his birthright; and it cannot therefore be necessary for your Committee to enlarge on its value, or to illustrate its effects. These would be undubitably confirmed by an appeal to our own commercial prosperity, no less than by the history of other trading nations, in which it has been ever found, that Commerce and Manufactures have flourished in free, and declined in despotic Countries. Report from the Committee on the State of the Woollen Manufacture of England, *Parliamentary Papers*, 1806, III, 7, 12

Dr Samuel Smiles (1812–1904), a Scottish shopkeeper's son, became the great apostle of such Victorian virtues as individualism and hard work. He produced a series of famous biographies of engineers and businessmen and a batch of quasi-philosophical works with such titles as *Self-Help* (1859), *Character* (1871), *Thrift* (1875), and *Duty* (1880). A 'best-seller', *Self-Help* was based on lectures given to a 'mutual improvement' class of Leeds workers in 1845. Its happy message was that by honest labour, determination, thrift, temperance, and 'courageous working' Victorian operatives could follow the road of the self-made industrialists. It was widely believed—and made Smiles a considerable fortune.

21 "Heaven helps those who help themselves" is a well-tried maxim, embodying in a small compass the results of vast human experience. The spirit of self-help is the root of all genuine growth in the individual; and, exhibited in the lives of many, it constitutes the true source of national vigour and strength. Help from without is often enfeebling in its effects, but help from within invariably invigorates. Whatever is done *for* men or classes, to a certain extent takes away the stimulus and necessity of doing for themselves; and where men are subjected to over-guidance and over-government, the inevitable tendency is to render them comparatively helpless.

Even the best institutions can give a man no active aid. Perhaps the utmost they can do is, to leave him *free* to develop himself and improve his individual condition. But in all times men have been prone to believe that their happiness and well-being were to be secured by means of institutions rather than by their own conduct. Hence the value of legislation as an agent in human advancement has always been greatly overestimated. To constitute the millionth part of a Legislature, by voting for one or two men once in three or five years, however conscientiously this duty may be performed, can exercise but little active influence upon any man's life and character. Moreover, it is every day becoming more clearly understood, that the function of Government is negative and restrictive, rather than positive and active; being resolvable principally into protection—protection of life, liberty, and property. Hence the chief "reforms" of the last fifty years have consisted mainly in abolitions and disenactments. But there is no power of law that can make the idle man industrious, the thriftless provident, or the drunken sober; though every individual can be each and all of these if he will, by the exercise of his own free powers of action and self-denial. Indeed all experience serves to prove that the worth and strength of a State depend far less upon the form of its institutions than upon the character of its men. For the nation is only the aggregate of individual conditions, and civilization itself is but a question of personal improvement.

National progress is the sum of individual industry, energy, and uprightness, as national decay is of individual idleness, selfishness, and vice. What we are accustomed to decry as great social evils, will, for the most part, be found to be only the outgrowth of our own perverted life; and though we may endeavour to cut them down and extirpate them by means of law, they will only spring up again with fresh luxuriance in some other form, unless the conditions of human life and character are radically improved. If this view be correct, then it follows that the highest patriotism and philanthropy consists, not so much in altering laws and modifying institutions, as in helping and stimulating men to elevate and improve themselves by their own free and independent action.　Samuel Smiles. *Self-Help*, 1859, 1–2

_____

The Spinning Inventions　The first Industrial Revolution consisted to a considerable extent of a series of major changes in the cotton industry—changes of technique, technology and organisation which gradually spread to other textile industries. The revolution in spinning, for long controlled by the monopolistic Sir Richard Arkwright (1732–92), proved to be the mechanical 'take-off'. Spinning and other early processes moved into the factory, promoting massive social changes. Mechanical spinning was an unskilled task, and the weavers' families often resisted the notion of factory life. The early masters were therefore obliged to seek 'immigrant' labour, and contrived a new 'apprenticeship' system to obtain the labour of children in the 'care' of the Poor Law authorities. Weavers' families now turned to the less sophisticated forms of weaving themselves. In the following extract Edward Baines looks back over the crucial and controversial story of the new spinning machines from the vantage-point of a nineteenth-century Liberal journalist-historian.

_____

22　Up to the year 1760, the machines used in the cotton manufacture in England were nearly as simple as those of India; though the loom was more strongly and perfectly constructed, and cards for combing the cotton had been adopted from the woollen manufacture.

The cotton manufacture, though rapidly increasing, could never have received such an extension as to become of great national importance, without the discovery of some method for producing a greater quantity and better quality of yarn with the same labour. None but the strong cottons, such as fustians and dimities, were as yet made in England, and for these the demand must always have been limited. Yet at present the demand exceeded the supply, and the modes of manufacture were such as greatly to impede the increase of production. The weaver was continually pressing upon the spinner. The processes of spinning and weaving were generally performed in the same cottage, but the weaver's own family could not supply him with a sufficient quantity of weft, and he had with much pains to collect it from neighbouring spinsters. Thus his time was wasted, and he was often subjected to high demands for an article, on which, as the demand exceeded the supply, the seller could put her own price.* A high and sustained price of yarn would indeed have attracted new hands to the employment, but such high price would itself have tended to keep down the rising manufacture, by making the goods too costly in comparison with other manufactures.

This difficulty was likely to be further aggravated by an invention which facilitated the process of weaving. In the year 1738, Mr. John Kay, a native of Bury, in Lancashire, then residing at Colchester, where the woollen manufacture was at that time carried on, suggested a mode of throwing the shuttle, which enabled the weaver to make nearly twice as much cloth as he could make before. The old mode was, to throw the shuttle with the hand, which required a constant extension of the hands to each side of the warp†. By the new plan, the lathe (in which the shuttle runs) was lengthened a foot at either end;

* Dr. Aikin says, "The weavers, in a scarcity of spinning, have sometimes been paid less for the weft than they paid the spinner, but durst not complain, much less abate the spinner, lest their looms should be unemployed."— *Hist. of Manchester*, p. 167. Mr. Guest, in his "History of the Cotton Manufacture", states that "it was no uncommon thing for a weaver to walk three or four miles in a morning, and call on five or six spinners, before he could collect weft to serve him for the remainder of the day; and when he wished to weave a piece in a shorter time than usual, a new ribbon, or a gown, was necessary, to quicken the exertions of the spinner". p. 12.

† In the first print of Hogarth's admirable series, "Industry and Idleness", where the two apprentices are seen at their looms, the old form of shuttle and lathe is represented: the industrious apprentice has the shuttle in his hand, ready to throw it; and the shuttle of the idle apprentice hangs dangling by the thread at the end of the lathe, affording a plaything for the cat, whilst the lad sleeps.

and, by means of two strings attached to the opposite ends of the lathe, and both held by a peg in the weaver's hand, he, with a slight and sudden pluck, was able to give the proper impulse to the shuttle. The shuttle thus impelled was called the *Fly-shuttle*, and the peg was called the *picking-peg*, (i.e. the *throwing* peg). This simple contrivance was a great saving of time and exertion to the weaver, and enabled one man to weave the widest cloth, which had before required two persons. "Mr. Kay brought this ingenious invention to his native town, and introduced it among the woollen weavers, in the same year, but it was not much used among the cotton weavers until 1760. In that year Mr. Robert Kay, of Bury, son of Mr. John Kay, invented the *drop-box*, by means of which the weaver can at pleasure use any one of three shuttles, each containing a different coloured weft, without the trouble of taking them from and replacing them in the lathe".*

These inventions, like every other invention which has contributed to the extraordinary advance of the cotton manufacture, were opposed by the workmen, who feared that they would lose their employment; and such was the persecution and danger to which John Kay was exposed, that he left his native country, and went to reside in Paris.

It has been seen, that the great impediment to the further progress of the manufacture was the impossibility of obtaining an adequate supply of yarn. The one-thread wheel, though turning from morning till night in thousands of cottages, could not keep pace either with the weaver's shuttle, or with the demand of the merchant.

The one-thread wheel, though much improved from the rude teak-wood wheel used in India, . . . was an extremely slow mode of spinning. . . .

The yarn was spun by two processes, called *roving* and *spinning*. In the first, the spinner took the short fleecy rolls in which

---

* Guest, p. 8. Mr. Guest derived his information on these points "from a manuscript lent to him by Mr. Samuel Kay, of Bury, son of Mr. Robert Kay, the inventor of the drop-box". p. 30.

the cotton was stripped off the hand-cards, applied them suc-
cessively to the spindle, and, whilst with one hand she turned
the wheel, and thus made the spindle revolve, with the other
she drew out the cardings, which, receiving a slight twist from
the spindle, were made into thick threads called rovings, and
wound upon the spindle so as to form cops. In the second process, the roving was spun into yarn: the operation was similar,
but the thread was drawn out finer, and received much more
twist. It will be seen that this instrument only admitted of one
thread being spun at a time by one pair of hands: and the
slowness of the operation, and consequent expensiveness of the
yarn formed a great obstacle to the establishment of a new
manufacture.

Genius stepped in to remove the difficulty, and gave wings
to a manufacture which had been creeping on the earth. A
mechanical contrivance was invented, by which twenty, fifty, a
hundred, or even a thousand threads could be spun at once by
a single pair of hands!

The authorship of this splendid invention, like that of the art
of printing, has been the subject of much doubt and contro-
versy; and by far the greater number of writers have subscribed
the honour to an individual, who, though possessed of extraordinary talent and merit, was certainly not the original inventor. Sir Richard Arkwright is generally believed, even to
the present day, to have invented the mode of *spinning by
rollers*. . . .

The inventor of the mode of *spinning by rollers* was JOHN
WYATT, of Birmingham. . . .

. . . This is the invention ascribed to Sir Richard Arkwright,
and on which his renown for mechanical genius mainly rests.
It will be found, however, that the process had previously been
described, with the utmost distinctness, in the specification of
the machine invented by John Wyatt, and that cotton had for
some years been spun by those machines. The patent for the
invention was taken out, in the year 1738, in the name of Lewis
Paul, a foreigner, with whom Mr. Wyatt had connected him-

self in partnership, and the name of John Wyatt only appears as a witness; but there is other evidence to show that the latter was really the inventor. The reason why Paul was allowed to take out the patent can only be conjectured; it may have been, that Wyatt was then in embarrassed circumstances.

In pursuing the history of spinning by rollers, we come now to the successful introduction of that invention by Sir Richard Arkwright, who, though not entitled to all the merit which has been claimed for him possessed very high inventive talent, as well as an unrivalled sagacity in estimating at their true value the mechanical contrivances of others, in combining them together, perfecting them, arranging a complete series of machinery, and constructing the factory system—itself a vast and admirable machine, which has been the source of great wealth, both to individuals and to the nation.

Richard Arkwright rose by the force of his natural talents from a very humble condition in society. He was born at Preston on the 23rd of December, 1732, of poor parents: being the youngest of thirteen children, his parents could only afford to give him an education of the humblest kind, and he was scarcely able to write. He was brought up to the trade of a barber at Kirkham and Preston, and established himself in that business at Bolton in the year 1760. Having become possessed of a chemical process for dyeing human hair,* which in that day (when wigs were universal) was of considerable value, he travelled about collecting hair, and again disposing of it when dyed. In 1761, he married a wife from Leigh, and the connexions he thus formed in that town are supposed to have afterwards brought him acquainted with Highs's experiments in making spinning machines. He himself manifested a strong bent for experiments in mechanics, which he is stated to have followed with so much devotedness as to have neglected his

---

* I have no means of knowing whether this secret was a discovery of his own, or was communicated to him. Mr. Guest says, he "possessed" the secret; Mr. Culloch, that he "discovered" it.

business and injured his circumstances. His natural disposition was ardent, enterprising, and stubbornly persevering: his mind was as coarse as it was bold and active, and his manners were rough and unpleasing.

In 1767, Arkwright fell in with Kay, the clockmaker, at Warrington, whom he employed to bend him some wires, and turn him some pieces of brass. From this it would seem that Arkwright was then experimenting in mechanics; and it has been said, that he was endeavouring to produce perpetual motion.* He entered into conversation with the clockmaker, and called upon him repeatedly; and at length Kay, according to his own account, told him of Highs's scheme of spinning by rollers. Kay adds, in his evidence, that Arkwright induced him to make a model of Highs's machine, and took it away. It is certain that from this period Arkwright abandoned his former business, and devoted himself to the construction of the spinning machine; and also, that he persuaded Kay to go with him first to Preston and afterwards to Nottingham, binding him in a bond to serve him at a certain rate of wages for a stipulated term. The particulars of what passed between Arkwright and Kay rest wholly on the evidence of the latter; but there is no doubt that Kay was thus engaged to accompany Arkwright, and that he worked for him some time at Nottingham. Those who believe in the invention of Highs find in this fact, combined with Highs's own evidence, a very strong presumption in its favour: but those who disbelieve it may adopt the conjecture, that Arkwright, not being a practical mechanic, engaged the clockmaker to construct the apparatus he had himself contrived. The statement of Arkwright, in the "Case" drawn up to be submitted to parliament, was, that "after many years' intense and painful application, he invented, about the year 1768, his present method of spinning cotton, but upon very different principles from any invention that had gone before it". It is true that Arkwright had been experimenting in mechanics,

*Aikin and Enfield's *General Biography*, Vol. I. p. 391.

but there is no evidence to shew that he had ever thought of making a spinning machine before his interview with Kay at Warrington.

Kay appears not to have been able to make the whole machine, and therefore "he and Arkwright applied to Mr. Peter Atherton, afterwards of Liverpool", (then probably an instrument maker at Warrington), "to make the spinning engine; but from the poverty of Arkwright's appearance, Mr. Atherton refused to undertake it, though afterwards, on the evening of the same day, he agreed to lend Kay a smith and watch-tool maker, to make the heavier part of the engine, and Kay undertook to make the clockmaker's part of it, and to instruct the workman. In this way Mr. Arkwright's first engine, for which he afterwards took out a patent, was made".*

Being altogether destitute of pecuniary means for prosecuting his invention, Arkwright repaired to his native place, Preston, and applied to a friend, Mr. John Smalley, a liquor-merchant and painter, for assistance. The famous contested election, at which General Burgoyne was returned, occurring during his visit, Arkwright voted; but the wardrobe of the future knight was in so tattered a condition, that a number of persons subscribed to put him into decent plight to appear at the poll-room. His spinning machine was fitted up in the parlour of the house belonging to the Free Grammar School, which was lent by the head-master to Mr. Smalley for the purpose.† The latter was so well convinced of the utility of the machine, that he joined Arkwright with heart and purse.

In consequence of the riots which had taken place in the neighbourhood of Blackburn, on the invention of Hargreaves's spinning jenny in 1767, by which many of the machines were destroyed, and the inventor was driven from his native county

---

* Aikin and Enfield's "General Biography", Vol. I. p. 391. The authors profess to have obtained some of these facts from private sources; and Dr. Aikin's opportunities were good, as he resided at Warrington.

† These facts are stated on the authority of Nicholas Grimshaw, Esq., several times mayor of Preston, who has personal knowledge of them.

to Nottingham, Arkwright and Smalley, fearing similar out-
rages directed against their machine, went also to Nottingham,
accompanied by Kay. This town, therefore, became the cradle
of two of the greatest inventions in cotton spinning. Here the
adventurers applied for pecuniary aid to Messrs. Wright,
bankers, who made advances on condition of sharing in the
profits of the invention. But as the machine was not perfected
so soon as they had anticipated, the bankers requested Arkwright to obtain other assistance, and recommended him to
Mr. Samuel Need, of Nottingham. This gentleman was the
partner of Mr. Jedediah Strutt, of Derby,* the ingenious improver and patentee of the stocking-frame; and Mr. Strutt
having seen Arkwright's machine, and declared it to be an
admirable invention, only wanting an adaptation of some of
the wheels to each other, both Mr. Need and Mr. Strutt
entered into partnership with Arkwright.

Thus the pecuniary difficulties of this enterprising and
persevering man were terminated. He soon made his machine
practicable, and in 1769 he took out a patent. In the specification, which was enrolled on the 15th of July in that year, he
stated that he "had by great study and long application invented a new piece of machinery, never before found out,
practised, or used, for the making of weft or yarn from cotton,
flax, and wool; which would be of great utility to a great
many manufacturers, as well as to his Majesty's subjects in
general, by employing a great number of poor people in working the said machinery, and by making the said weft or yarn

---

* Mr. Strutt was brought up a farmer, but, having a passion for improvement and a mechanical genius, he succeeded in adapting the stocking-frame
to the manufacture of *ribbed* stockings, for which improvement he obtained
a patent. He established an extensive manufacture of ribbed stockings at
Derby, and, after his connexion with Mr. Arkwright, he erected cotton
works at Milford, near Belper: he raised his family to great wealth. Some
of the circumstances connected with Arkwright's settling at Nottingham,
were communicated by the late Mr. William Strutt, the highly gifted and
ingenious son of Mr. Jedediah Strutt, to the editor of the Beauties of England
and Wales. See vol. III. pp. 518, 541.

much superior in quality to any ever heretofore manufactured or made".

. . . Such is the original of the present water-frame and throstle. It was afterwards greatly improved by Arkwright himself; and, when horse-power was exchanged for water-power, the number of spindles in the frame was multiplied. The original machine was adapted only to perform the last operation in spinning, namely, reducing the rovings into yarn; but it was easily applicable to the process of roving itself, as will subsequently appear. It is remarkable that the inventor, in his application for a patent, described himself as "Richard Arkwright, of Nottingham, *clockmaker*".* He and his partners erected a mill at Nottingham, which was driven by horses; but this mode of turning the machinery being found too expensive, they built another mill on a much larger scale at Cromford, in Derbyshire, which was turned by a water wheel, and from this circumstance the spinning machine was called the *water-frame*.

The difficulty, delay, and expense which attended the completing of the invention, prove, at the very least, that Arkwright did not receive it from any other person a *perfect* machine. If he had seen either Wyatt's machine, or the model of that of Highs, he had still to perfect the details; and the determined assiduity and confidence with which he devoted himself to this undertaking, before the machine had ever been made to answer, show that he had sufficient mechanical capacity to appreciate its value, and sufficient talent and energy to make the invention practicable and profitable.

. . . The great demand for yarn, while the one-thread wheel was the only instrument for spinning, set other wits on contriving a substitute for it, besides those of Wyatt, Highs, and Arkwright.

We learn from the "Transactions of the Society for the En-

---

* This was certainly an untrue description, and Mr. Guest remarks upon it, that Arkwright "did not scruple to masquerade in the character and trade of John Kay".—Reply, p. 58.

couragement of Arts, Manufactures, and Commerce", that in 1783 the society had in its repositories models of the following spinning machines: "A Spinning Wheel, by Mr. John Webb, invented 1761. A Spinning Wheel, by Mr. Thomas Perrin, 1761. A Horizontal Spinning Wheel, by Mr. Wm. Harrison, 1764. A Spinning Wheel, by Mr. Perrin, 1765. A Spinning Wheel, by Mr. Garrat, 1766. A Spinning Wheel, by Mr. Garrat, 1767".* Between the establishment of the society in 1754 and the year 1783, it distributed £544. 12s. in premiums "for improving several machines used in manufactures, viz. the comb-pot, cards for wool and cotton, stocking frame, loom, machines for winding and doubling, and spinning wheels".† None of these inventions of spinning machines, however, succeeded. The compiler of the Transactions, writing in 1783, says, "From the best information hitherto obtained, it appears, that about the year 1764, a poor man, of the name of Hargreaves, employed in the cotton manufactury near Blackburn, in Lancashire, first made a machine in that county, which spun eleven threads; and that in the year 1770 he obtained a patent for the invention. The construction of this kind of machine, called a *Spinning Jenny*, has since been much improved, and is now at so high a degree of perfection, that one woman is thereby enabled with ease to spin a hundred threads of cotton at a time".‡

James Hargreaves, a weaver of Stand-hill, near Blackburn, was the author of the admirable invention noticed in this extract.¶ It has been generally supposed that the date of the

---

* Transactions of the Society of Arts, vol. I. pp. 314, 315.
† Ibid, vol I, p 26.
‡ Ibid, vol I, pp 33, 34.
¶ Mr. Guest prefers a claim on the part of Thomas Highs, of Leigh, to the invention of the spinning-jenny, as well as of the water-frame. After attentively considering the evidence adduced, I am of the opinion that it is quite insufficient to establish the claim. At the trial on Arkwright's patent, when Highs was examined pretty largely as to his inventions, he did not even allude to the jenny, which it is almost certain he would, to prove his great inventive talent, had he been the inventor. It is true that two men, named

invention was 1767, not 1764; and Arkwright, in his "Case", states the machine to have been made in 1767. It is, however, in the highest degree probable, that the jenny would not be at once perfected: its construction would probably occupy the author, who was a poor man, and had to work for his daily bread, some years: and as Hargreaves went to Nottingham in 1768, before which time his machine had not only been perfected, but its extraordinary powers so clearly proved, notwithstanding his efforts to keep it secret, as to expose him to persecution and the attacks of a mob, I am strongly disposed to think that the invention was conceived, and that the author began to embody it, as early as 1764.

Hargreaves, though illiterate and humble, must be regarded as one of the greatest inventors and improvers in the cotton manufacture. His principal invention, and one which shewed

Thomas Leather and Thomas Wilkinson, the one 69 and the other 75 years old when their evidence was taken, stated in 1823 and 1827, that they knew Highs, and that he made a spinning-jenny about the year 1763 or 1764. The former also stated, that the machine was called *jenny* after Highs's daughter Jane; and there is ample evidence that Highs had a daughter of that name. It is added, that Kay, the clockmaker, assisted in the construction of this machine, as well as in that of the water-frame. The last-mentioned circumstance leads me to the belief that the witnesses have confounded the two inventions. Moreover, as Highs undoubtedly made jennies at a later period, and also invented a double jenny with some new apparatus, this fact may have given rise to the belief that he was the original inventor. The recollections of two aged men, concerning precise dates, after the lapse of sixty years, and concerning the precise form of a machine seen by them in mere boyhood, are little to be relied upon, especially for the purpose of overturning the claims of a most ingenious man, the patentee of the invention, and whose pretensions were never disputed till the appearance of Mr. Guest's book. Highs, however, has a third claim as an inventor; he stated, on Arkwright's patent trial, that he made a *perpetual carding* in the year 1773, which was before any other person did the same thing. It is certain that he was an extremely ingenious man, and he continued to make spinning machines till he was disabled by a stroke of the palsy, about the year 1790. He was supported in his old age by the liberality of Peter Drinkwater, Esq., of Manchester, and others, and died on the 13th December 1803, aged eighty-four years.

high mechanical genius, was the jenny. The date of this invention was some years before Arkwright obtained the patent for his water-frame; and it differs so completely from that machine, and from Wyatt's, that there can be no suspicion of its being other than a perfectly original invention.

... Before quitting Lancashire, Hargreaves had made a few jennies for sale;* and the importance of the invention being universally appreciated, the interests of the manufacturers and weavers brought it into general use, in spite of all opposition. A desperate effort was, however, made in 1779—probably in a period of temporary distress—to put down the machine. A mob rose, and scoured the country for several miles round Blackburn, demolishing the jennies, and with them all the carding engines, water-frames, and every machine turned by water or horses. ... It may seem strange, that not merely the working classes, but even the middle and upper classes, entertained a great dread of machinery. Not perceiving the tendency of any invention which improved and cheapened the manufacture, to cause an extended demand for its products, and thereby to give employment to more hands than it superseded, those classes were alarmed lest the poor-rates should be burdened with workmen thrown idle. ...

... The two important inventions for spinning, of which the history has been traced, broke down the barrier which had so long obstructed the advance of the cotton manufacture. The new machines not only turned off a much greater quantity of yarn than had before been produced, but the yarn was also of a superior quality. The water-frame spun a hard and firm thread, calculated for warps; and from this time the warps of linen yarn were abandoned, and goods were, for the first time in this country, woven wholly of cotton. Manufactures of a finer and more delicate fabric were also introduced, especially calicoes, imitated from the Indian fabrics of that name. The jenny was peculiarly adapted for spinning weft; so that the

* It is mentioned by Mr. Kennedy, that Crompton, the inventor of the mule, "learnt to spin upon a jenny of Hargreaves's make", in 1769.

two machines, instead of coming in conflict, were brought into use together. . . .

. . . The factory system in England takes its rise from this period. Hitherto the cotton manufacture had been carried on almost entirely in the houses of the workmen. . . . But the water-frame, the carding engine, and the other machines which Arkwright brought out in a finished state, required both more space than could be found in a cottage, and more power than could be applied by the human arm. Their weight also rendered it necessary to place them in strongly-built mills, and they could not be advantageously turned by any power then known but that of water.

During the period that has now passed under review, Hargreaves and Arkwright had established the Cotton Manufacture by their spinning machines; but those machines were not adapted for the finer qualities of yarn. . . . This defect in the spinning machinery was remedied by the invention of another machine, called the *Mule*, or the *Mule Jenny*, from its combining the principles of Arkwright's water-frame and Hargreaves's jenny. . . .

This excellent machine, which has superseded the jenny, and to a considerable extent the water-frame, and which has carried the cotton manufacture to a perfection it could not otherwise have attained, was invented by Samuel Crompton, a weaver, of respectable character and moderate circumstances, living at Hall-in-the-Wood, near Bolton. The date of the invention has been generally stated to be 1775, but . . . his own account is decisive: he says in a letter to a friend:—"In regard to the mule, the date of its being first completed was in the year 1779. . . .". . . . Edward Baines. *History of the Cotton Manufacture in Great Britain*, 1835, 115–19, 121, 147–52, 153–6, 159–60, 163–4, 184, 197–9

Samuel Crompton (1753–1827) had a career more typical of the majority of early textile inventors than the great financial

and 'social' success of Sir Richard Arkwright. His 'mule'
helped to make many fortunes, but only briefly helped the
simple weaver; Crompton lacked the barber's flair for business.
Andrew Ure based the following note on a paper read to the
Manchester Literary and Philosophical Society on 20 February
1830 by John Kennedy (1769–1855), Crompton's benefactor
and 'one of the most scientific manufacturers of the kingdom'.
The mule became the dominant spinning machine, particularly when used in connection with steam power; it thus helped
to extend the factory system at a vital stage of its development.

---

23 Samuel Crompton was born on the 3rd December, 1753,
at Firwood, in Lancashire, where his father held a farm of
small extent; and, according to the custom of those days,
employed a portion of his time in carding, spinning, and weaving. Hall-in-the-Wood, a picturesque cottage near Bolton,
became the residence of the family during the son's infancy,
and the memorable scene of his juvenile inventions. His father
died when he was very young. The care of his education de-
volved on his mother, a pious woman, who lived in a retired
manner, and imparted her own sincere and contemplative turn
of mind to her son. In all his dealings through life Samuel was
strictly honest, patient, and humane.

When about sixteen years old, namely, about 1769, he learnt
to spin upon a jenny of Hargreaves' make, and occasionally
wore what he had spun. Being dissatisfied with the quality of
his yarn, he began to consider how it might be improved, and
was thus naturally led to the construction of his novel spinning
machine. He commenced this task when twenty-one years of
age, and devoted five years to its execution. As he was not,
properly speaking, a mechanic, and possessed only such simple
tools as his little earnings at the jenny and the loom enabled
him to procure, he proceeded but slowly with the construction
of his mule, but still in a progressive manner highly creditable
to his dexterity and perseverance.

He often said that what annoyed him most was that he was

G

not allowed to employ his little invention by himself in his garret; for, as he got a better price for his yarns than his neighbours did, he was naturally supposed to have mounted some superior mechanism, and hence became an object of the prying curiosity of the country people for miles around, many of whom climbed up at the windows to see him at his work. He erected a screen in order to obstruct their view, but he continued to be so incommoded by crowds of visiters, that he resolved at last to get rid of the vexatious mystery by disclosing the whole contrivances before a number of gentlemen and others, who chose to subscribe a guinea a-piece for the inspection. In this way he collected about £50, and was hence enabled to construct another similar machine, upon a better and larger plan. The first contained no more than thirty to forty spindles.

About the year 1802 Mr. Kennedy and Mr. Lee, of Manchester, set on foot a subscription for him, whereby they obtained £500; which formed a little capital for the increase of his small manufactory at Bolton. As a weaver, also, he displayed great ingenuity, and erected several looms for the fancy work of that town. Being fond of music, he built himself an organ, with which he entertained his leisure hours in his cottage. Though his means were slender, he was such a master of domestic economy, as to be always in easy circumstances. In 1812 he made a survey of all the cotton districts in England, Scotland, and Ireland, and obtained an estimate of the number of spindles at work upon his mule principle—then amounting to between four and five millions, and in 1829 to about seven. On his return, he laid the result of his inquiries before his generous friends Messrs. Kennedy and Lee, with a suggestion that Parliament might possibly grant him some recompense for the national advantages derived from his invention. A memorial was accordingly drawn up, in the furtherance of which the late George Duckworth, Esq., of Manchester, and the principal manufacturers in the kingdom, to whom his merits were made known, took a lively interest. He went to London himself with the memorial, and had the satisfaction to see a bill pass through parliament for a grant to him of £5000, without deduction for fees or charges.

This sum was advanced to his sons in order to carry on a bleaching concern, for the support of the family. But they mismanaged the business, lost the money, and became bankrupt, reducing their father and sister to poverty. Mr. Kennedy, with Messrs. Hicks and Rothwell, the eminent civil engineers of Bolton, and a few other gentlemen, raised by a second subscription, a sum which purchased for Mr. Crompton a life annuity of £63. He enjoyed this benevolent pittance only two years, for he died on the 26th of January, 1827, leaving his daughter without any provision. Andrew Ure. *The Cotton Manufacture of Great Britain*, 1836, I, 263–5

_____

The Power-Loom   The idea of a mechanical loom was an old one; Baines notices that in 1678 the Royal Society heard of M. de Gennes' 'new engine to make linen cloth without the help of an artificer'. Another Frenchman, James de Vaucanson (1709–82) constructed a swivel-loom, which was apparently used in Gartside's Manchester factory in 1765. Cumbersome and needing constant attention, such early looms were not successful. However, the spate of spinning inventions made improved weaving machinery increasingly desirable. The first 'break-through' was made by the Rev Dr Edmund Cartwright (1743–1823), the Rector of Goadby Marwood in Leicestershire and brother of the Radical agitator John Cartwright, in 1785. Cartwright described his work in the following letter to Dugald Bannatyne (originally published in the *Encyclopaedia Britannica*). He failed in a weaving venture (powered by a bull) at Doncaster and lost money on both his weaving and woolcombing inventions, but in 1809 received a Parliamentary grant of £10,000. His own account is here reprinted by Richard Guest, an early historian of the cotton industry.

_____

24   Happening to be at Matlock, in the summer of 1784, I fell in company with some gentlemen of Manchester, when the conversation turned on Arkwright's spinning machinery. One of the company observed, that as soon as Arkwright's patent expired, so many mills would be erected, and so much cotton spun, that hands never could be found to weave it. To this observation I replied that Arkwright must then set his wits to work to invent a weaving mill. This brought on a conversation on the subject, in which the Manchester gentlemen unanimously agreed that the thing was impracticable; in defence of their opinion, they adduced arguments which I certainly was incompetent to answer or even to comprehend, being totally ignorant of the subject, having never at that time seen a person weave. I controverted, however, the impracticability of the thing, by remarking that there had lately been exhibited in London, an automation figure, which played at chess. Now you will not assert, gentlemen, said I, that it is more difficult to construct a machine that shall weave, than one which shall make all the variety of moves which are required in that complicated game.

Some little time afterwards, a particular circumstance recalling this conversation to my mind, it struck me, that, as in plain weaving, according to the conception I then had of the business, there could only be three movements, which were to follow each other in succession, there would be little difficulty in producing and repeating them. Full of these ideas, I immediately employed a carpenter and smith to carry them into effect. As soon as the machine was finished, I got a weaver to put in the warp, which was of such materials as sail cloth is usually made of. To my great delight, a piece of cloth, such as it was, was the produce.

As I had never before turned my thoughts to anything mechanical, either in theory or practice, nor had ever seen a loom at work, or knew anything of its construction, you will readily suppose that my first loom must have been a most rude piece of machinery.

The warp was placed perpendicularly, the reed fell with a force of at least half a hundred weight, and the springs which threw the shuttle were strong enough to have thrown a Congreve rocket. In short, it required the strength of two powerful men to work the machine at a slow rate, and only for a short time. Conceiving in my great simplicity, that I had accomplished all that was required, I then secured what I thought a most valuable property, by a patent, 4 April, 1785. This being done, I then condescended to see how other people wove; and you will guess my astonishment, when I compared their easy modes of operation with mine. Availing myself, however, of what I then saw, I made a loom in its general principles, nearly as they are now made. But it was not till the year 1787, that I completed my invention, when I took out my last weaving patent, August 1st of that year. Richard Guest. *A Compendious History of the Cotton Manufacture*, 1823, 44–5

Steam Power Experiments with steam power had been made since the early seventeenth century, and David Ramseye was granted patents in 1630 for steam-powered mine pumps. The 2nd Marquess of Worcester explained the importance of steam in his *Century of Inventions* (1663), but it was not until late in the century that Thomas Savery (c 1650–1715) successfully built steam engines to drain Cornish mines. Savery's patent of 1698 was followed in 1705 by another, jointly owned by Savery and the great Devonshire engineer Thomas Newcomen (1663–1729). Apart from an improvement by Henry Beighton (1686–1743) in 1717, the pioneer steam engine was scarcely altered until the major developments made by the Glasgow mechanic James Watt (1736–1819) and his Birmingham partner Matthew Boulton (1728–1809). The achievements of Boulton and Watt are here described by Edward Baines.

25 Amazing as is the progress which had taken place in the cotton manufacture prior to 1700, it would soon have found a check upon its further extension, if a power more efficient than water had not been discovered to move the machinery. The building of mills in Lancashire must have ceased, when all the available fall of the streams had been appropriated. The manufacture might indeed have spread to other counties, as it has done to some extent; but it would not have flourished in any district where coal as well as water was not to be found; and the diffusion of the mills over a wide space would have been unfavourable to the division of labour, the perfection of machine-making, and the cheapness of conveyance.

At this period a power was happily discovered, of almost universal application and unlimited extent, adapted to every locality where fuel was cheap, and available both to make machines and to work them, both to produce goods, and to convey them by land and water. This power was the *steam-engine*, which, though not an invention of that age, was first made of great and extensive utility by the genius of James Watt.

. . . James Watt, a native of Greenock, was brought up as a maker of philosophical instruments in Glasgow and London, and settled in Glasgow in 1757. He was appointed instrument maker to the university, and thus became acquainted with Dr. Black, professor of medicine and lecturer on chemistry in that institution, who, about this time, published his important and beautiful discovery of latent heat. The knowledge of this doctrine led Watt to reflect on the prodigious waste of heat in the steam-engine, where steam was used merely for the purpose of creating a vacuum in the cylinder under the piston, and for that end was condensed in the cylinder itself,—the piston being then forced down solely by atmospheric pressure. The cylinder was therefore alternately warmed by the steam, and cooled by the admission of cold water to condense the steam; and when the steam was readmitted after the cooling process, much of it was instantly condensed by the cold cylinder, and a great waste of the steam took place: of course, there was an equal waste of the fuel which produced the steam, and this rendered the use of the machine very costly.

It happened that Watt was employed, in the year 1763, to repair a small working model of Newcomen's steam-engine for Professor Anderson. He saw its defects, and studied how to remedy them. He perceived the vast capabilities of an engine, moved by so powerful an agent as steam, if that agent could be properly applied. His scientific knowledge, as well as his mechanical ingenuity, was called forth; all the resources of his sagacious and philosophical mind were devoted to the task; and after years of patient labour and costly experiments, which nearly exhausted his means, he succeeded in removing every difficulty, and making the steam-engine the most valuable instrument for the application of power, which the world has ever known.

It is not a little remarkable that his patent, "for lessening the consumption of steam and fuel in fire engines", should have been taken out in the same year as Arkwright's patent for spinning with rollers, namely, 1769—one of the most brilliant eras in the annals of British genius;—when Black and Priestley were making their great discoveries in science; when Hargreaves, Arkwright, and Watt revolutionized the processes of manufacturers, when Smeaton and Brindley executed prodigies of engineering art; when the senate was illuminated by Burke and Fox, Chatham and Mansfield; when Johnson and Goldsmith, Reid and Beattie, Hume, Gibbon, and Adam Smith, adorned the walks of philosophy and letters.

The patent of 1769 did not include all Watt's improvements. He connected himself in 1775 with Mr. Boulton, of Soho, Birmingham, a gentleman of wealth, enterprise, and mechanical talent; and, having made still further improvements in the steam-engine, an Act of parliament was passed in the same year, vesting in him "the sole use and property of certain steam-engines (or fire-engines) of his invention, throughout his majesty's dominions", for the extraordinary term of twenty-five years.* So comprehensive was the Act, that it prevented others

---

* The reasons for this great favour shown to Mr. Watt are thus stated in the Act: "James Watt has expended great part of his fortune in making experiments to improve steam-engines; but on account of the difficulties in execution, could not complete his invention before the end of 1774, when he finished some large engines, which have succeeded. In order to make those

from making steam-engines which contained improvements of
their own, if their engines condensed the steam in a separate
vessel: this was the foundation of Watt's improvements, and it
was so great an improvement, that no person could without
immense disadvantage dispense with it. Watt, therefore, took
up his position in a narrow pass, which he was able to defend
against a host; and he kept the whole business of making steam-
engines to himself, deterring all invaders of his privilege by
instantly commencing prosecutions. He enjoyed his patent for
more than thirty years, from 1769 to 1800: and, though it was
probably unproductive for the first ten years, it afterwards
produced him a large fortune, so that he retired from business
a wealthy man, on the expiration of the exclusive privilege.
The monopoly was much more extended than any legislature
ought to have granted; but it must be allowed that no man
could have better deserved or better used it.

Watt laboured incessantly to perfect this important and
complicated engine, and took out three other patents in 1781,
1782, and 1784, for great and essential improvements. . . .

Up to the time of Watt, and indeed up to the year 1782, the
steam-engine had been almost exclusively used to pump water
out of mines. He perfected its mechanism, so as to adapt it to
the production of rotative motion and the working of machinery;
and the first engine of that kind was erected by Boulton and
Watt at Bradley iron-works, in that year. The first engine
which they made for a cotton mill was in the works of Messrs.
Robinsons, of Papplewick, in Nottinghamshire, in the year

engines with accuracy, at moderate prices, a large sum must be previously
expended in mills and apparatus; and as several years and repeated proofs
will be required before the public can be fully convinced of their interest to
adopt the invention, the term of the patent may elapse before he is recom-
pensed. By furnishing mechanical power at less expense, and in more convenient forms than hitherto, his engines may be of great utility in many
great works and manufactures, yet he cannot carry his invention into that
complete execution that will render it of the highest utility of which it is
capable, unless the term be prolonged, and his property in the invention
secured in Scotland, as well as in England and the colonies".

1785. An atmospheric engine had been put up by Messrs. Arkwright and Simpson for their cotton mill on Shude-hill, Manchester, in 1783: but it was not till 1789 that a steam-engine was erected by Boulton and Watt in that town for cotton spinning, when they made one for Mr. Drinkwater: nor did Sir Richard Arkwright adopt the new invention till 1790, when he had one of Boulton and Watt's engines put up in a cotton mill at Nottingham. In Glasgow, the first steam-engine for cotton spinning was set up for Messrs. Scott and Stevenson, in 1792. So truly had it been predicted in the Act of 1775, that "several years, and repeated proofs, would be required before the public would be fully convinced of their interest to adopt the invention". But when the unrivalled advantages of the steam-engine, as a moving force for all kinds of machinery, came to be generally known, it was rapidly adopted throughout the kingdom, and for every purpose requiring great and steady power. The number of engines in use in Manchester, before the year 1800, was probably 32, and their power 430 horse; and at Leeds there were 20 engines, of 270 horse-power.*

By some writers, who have not remarked the wonderful spring which had been given to the cotton manufacture before the steam-engine was applied to spinning machinery, too great stress has been laid upon this engine, as if it had almost created the manufacture. This was not the case. The *spinning machinery* created the cotton manufacture. But this branch of industry has unquestionably been extended by means of the steam-engine far beyond the limit which it could otherwise have reached. . . .

The spirit of improvement, which had carried the spinning machinery to so high a degree of perfection, was next directed to the *weaving* department, and did not rest till that operation, as well as spinning, was performed by machinery. Edward Baines. *History of the Cotton Manufacture in Great Britain*, 1835, 220-1, 222-5, 226-7, 228

*Farey on the Steam Engine, p. 654.

Messrs Boulton & Watt enjoyed an enormous success with their improved steam engines. The firm's engineers superintended the erection of each engine and, until their patent expired in 1800, the firm collected a fee equivalent to one-third of the coal saved by their engine as compared to a Newcomen type. In this passage Ure describes the introduction of the new engines into the Lancashire cotton industry.

---

26 The oldest cotton mill in Manchester is that on Shude Hill, which was erected about the year 1780, by Messrs. Arkwright, Simpson, and Whitenburgh; being one of the numerous speculations into which the active author of the factory system entered. It was remarkable for its motive power, which was a hydraulic wheel furnished with water by a single-stroke atmospheric pumping steam-engine.

In his valuable paper on the rise and progress of the cotton trade, Mr. Kennedy justly remarks that the introduction of Watt's admirable steam-engine imparted new life to this business. Its inexhaustible power and uniform regularity of motion supplied what was most urgently wanted at the time; and the scientific principles and excellent workmanship displayed in its construction, led those who were interested in this trade to make many and great improvements in their machines and apparatus for bleaching, dyeing, and printing, as well as for spinning. Had it not been for this new accession of power and scientific mechanism, the cotton trade would have been stunted in its growth, and, compared with its present state, must have become an object of only minor importance in a national point of view.*

The first instance of the application of steam to cotton spinning was at Papplewick, in Nottinghamshire, where Boulton and Watt erected an engine in 1785, for the spirited proprietors Messrs. Robinson. In 1787, they erected one engine for Messrs. Puls, cotton spinners, at Warrington, and three others in

---

* *Memoirs of the Literary and Philosophical Society of Manchester*, vol. III, 2nd series.

Nottingham. Hitherto the hosiery trade gave the principal demand for power-spun cotton. It was not till 1789, that the calico trade of Manchester gave birth to a factory moved by steam, when Mr. Drinkwater mounted a handsome mill with one of Watt's engines. In 1790 Sir Richard Arkwright followed his example, in a mill erected at Nottingham. The same year a second engine, for cotton spinning, was fitted up in Manchester, for Mr. Simpson, and also at Papplewick for Messrs. Robinson. It ought to be mentioned that Sir Richard had tried steam power at an earlier period, but out of an ill-judged economy, he had adopted Newcomen's machines, rendered rotatory by a heavy fly-wheel; but seeing his error, he replaced them by engines of Watt's construction. Andrew Ure. *The Cotton Manufacture of Great Britain*, 1836, I, 273–4

Boulton had not been Watt's first partner: Dr John Roebuck, who first backed him, had been bankrupted in 1773. Watt moved to Birmingham in 1774 and the celebrated firm of Boulton & Watt commenced operations in 1775. Originally many parts were made by the ironmaster John Wilkinson, but his dishonesty led the partners to establish their own great Soho foundry near Birmingham in 1795. The range of the firm's interests is demonstrated by the following extracts from the Boulton & Watt correspondence in Birmingham City Library. Boulton's firm was continued by his son, Matthew Robinson Boulton (d 1842), the author of the last letter.

27 The other day I had a letter from Mr. James Black offering his services to the albion Mill Company. I told him we did not intermeddle with the direction, & that a person was appointed chief Clerk and Manager, that you & Mr. Wyat were principals in the direction, & that I would write to you to lay any proposal he might make before the Committee. I took this method because I think I once heard some thing not very favourable of him & from my commission with his Brother the Doctor did not chuse to give him a flat denial, I think at any rate we would

not saddle ourselves with expensive servants untill we know better what we are about—Mr. Rennie writes me that the Messrs. Diggens of Chichester have applied to him to know our terms for an Engine able to work two pairs of Stones, which I have wrote to him. As these people are very great corn merchants, they would be a desirable connection in the A.M. [?]. I therefore desired Mr. R. to mention to Mr. Wyat that he might try if they would come in as partners. Without we have some men of character that understand the business among us we shall do no good. . . .

James Watt to Mr Matthews, 1 September 1785

The nozles & working Gear of your Engine were sent off from hence last week, and I hope next week to send off the remainder of the materials, they would have been ready in the beginning of the week, but this having been Handsworth wake few of our men have been at work. James Law who we propose to put your Engine together I expect here to morrow, and shall send off for you as soon as possible but as he has been away these four months will probably wish to spend some days with his wife. The character I have got from Cornwall of S. Hancock is unfavourable, he is said to be quite incapable of putting the Engine together. "He worked as a carpenter at Wheel Maid Rotative Engine, and wrought the engine sometime afterwards, he can work tolerably as a Carpenter & manage the Engine pretty well, but is not to be depended upon either for regularity Sobriety or *honesty*". As he has been used to the work he may be usefull in assisting at putting the Engine together, and to work it untill somebody else is taught. And as the Character given may be in part dictated by partiality, I forbear to say the worst I have heard of him, but wish you to be on your guard, and make your own observations.

James Watt to Messrs Walker & Ley, 8 October 1785

I have not forgot you; but have done all I could to push your work forward. I hear from Birsham that your cyl^{rs}. and condenser were sent off to the canal a week ago and I hope are now arrived with you. The things here are going on as fast as they can. The matter which is most behind is the Boiler, in plates for which we were very disapointed & afterwards found some difficulty in procuring a man to make it such workmen being scarce here. We have at last got one he is at work upon it, and will not be long about it.

I am obliged to set out for London tomorrow where I shall be obliged to stay till the end of next week but have left strict orders to push on your work & hope by my return to find it mostly done.

James Watt to George Robinson, 11 October 1785

. . . R. Ewart is just return'd from Liverpool & will set out tomorrow or Tuesday—

He has been desired by Mr. Meyers of Liverpool, with whom we have had some correspondance upon the subject of Engines, to procure for him an Estimate of a 12 Horse Engine with & without the flywheel—Their present fly is 14/ft diam^r— Your answer may as well be sent directly to Mr. Meyers, but I should have a copy of the estimate for my government when I go to Liverpool, which I intend to do before leaving this neighbourhood—

You will have been informed by Mr. Watt of the submission of Bateman & Co. whose defeat leave us now without competitors in this quarter & every exertion should be made to supply the numerous Engines that are likely to be wanted in this part of the Kingdom. Bateman & Co. were driving a roaring Trade & had at the time they were served with Inquisitions a great number of orders in hand—Indeed the field opened for us is very extensive & we shall have to reproach ourselves only if we do not take every advantage of this favorable opportunity —One great difficiency in our arrangements is the want of a good workman of rather more intelligence than the common run of our Engineers, to be constantly resident here, he might be employed very advantageously in superintending the erec-

tion of new [Engines?] & the repairs of those now at work.[?]
has disgusted several of our Customers,[?] I fear is incorrigible,
many of them complain of the want of a person to whom they
could address themselves in case of any accident which at
present they are obliged to get repaired under the direction of
their own Engine Men or by Bateman & Co. We should therefore as soon as possible endeavour to find a proper person for
this department.

Lee's boiler leaks considerably in some of the Joints exposed
to the flues and he is obliged to use the old one, while the other
is repairing.

This circumstance should be pointed out to Horton. . . .

M. Robinson Boulton to J. Southern, 29 May 1796

The Organisers   The great entrepreneurs of the Industrial
Revolution came from many varied backgrounds. Robert Peel
(1723–95) was a yeoman near Blackburn when he started a
famous family business. He began with a calico establishment
at Blackburn in the 1760s and later became a major industrialist at Burton. His family was well rewarded for the enterprise here described by Baines: the yeoman's son became a
Tory squire, MP, and baronet, and his grandson became a
Conservative prime minister.

28   The introduction of calico printing into Lancashire is
ascribed to the Messrs. Clayton, of Bamber Bridge, near
Preston, who began the business on a small scale as early as the
year 1764. They were followed, and with greater vigour, by
Mr. Robert Peel, the grandfather of the present right honourable Sir Robert Peel, bart., late secretary of state. Mr. Peel was
originally a yeoman farming his own estate, and lived at Cross,
afterwards called Peel-fold, near Blackburn. Being of an active
and enterprising disposition, he began the manufacture of
cotton, and he is mentioned as one of the first persons who tried
the carding cylinder. He also took up the printing business, and
I have been informed by a member of his family that he made

his first experiments secretly in his own house; that the cloth, instead of being calendered, was ironed by a female of the family; and that the pattern was a parsley leaf. Stimulated by the success of his experiments, he embarked in the printing business with small means and convenience, and shortly after removed to Brookside, a village two miles from Blackburn. Here he carried on the business for some years with the aid of his sons; and by great application, skill, and enterprise, the concern was made eminently prosperous. His eldest son, Robert, afterwards created a baronet, possessed strong talents, which he devoted assiduously to business from an early age, and thus contributed much to the success of the printing, spinning and manufacturing businesses; and in each of these branches the Peels soon took a lead in Lancashire. They eagerly adopted every improvement suggested by others, and many improvements originated in their own extensive establishments. As the elder Mr. Peel had several sons, Robert quitted his father's concern about 1773, and established himself with his uncle, Mr. Haworth, and his future father-in-law, Mr. William Yates, at Bury, where the cotton spinning and printing trades were carried on for many years with pre-eminent success, and on a most extensive scale, and are, indeed, continued, though in other hands, to the present day. Mr. Peel, the father, with his other sons, and another Mr. Yates, established the print-works at Church, and had also large works at Burnley, Salley Abbey, and Foxhill-bank, and spinning mills at Altham, and afterwards at Burton-upon-Trent, in Staffordshire. So widely did these concerns branch out, and so liberally and skilfully were they conducted, that they not only brought immense wealth to the proprietors, but set an example to the whole of the cotton trade, and trained up many of the most successful printers and manufacturers in Lancashire. The history of the two houses, the Peels of Bury, and the Peels of Church, is, indeed, the history of the spinning, weaving, and printing of Lancashire for many years.   Edward Baines. *History of the Cotton Manufacture in Great Britain*, 1835, 262–4.

Inevitably, there were casualties among the risk-taking entrepreneurs of the Industrial Revolution. One was the venturesome William Radcliffe [see p 46] of Stockport. In the following extract he describes his own entry into the ranks of the employers. His customer Samuel Oldknow (1756–1828), a former tradesman, built the famous Mellor factory estate in 1793, staffing his mills largely with 'apprentice' children.

---

29 The principal estates being gone from the family, my father resorted to the common but never failing resource for subsistence at that period, viz.—the loom for men, and the cards and hand-wheel for women and boys. He married a spinster, (in my etymology of the word) and my mother taught me (while too young to weave) to earn my bread by carding and spinning cotton, winding linen or cotton weft for my father and elder brothers at the loom, until I became of sufficient age and strength for my father to put me into a loom. After the practical experience of a few years, any young man who was industrious and careful, might then from his earnings as a weaver, lay by sufficient to set him up as a manufacturer, and though but few of the great body of the weavers had the courage to embark in the attempt, I was one of those few. Availing myself of the improvements that came out while I was in my teens, by the time I was married (at the age of 24, in 1785) with my little savings, and a practical knowledge of every process from the cotton-bag to the piece of cloth, such as carding by hand or by the engine, spinning by the hand-wheel or jenny, winding, warping, sizing, looming the web, and weaving either by hand or fly-shuttle, I was ready to commence business for myself; and by the year 1789, I was well established, and employed many hands both in spinning and weaving, as a master-manufacturer.

From 1789 to 1794, my chief business was the sale of muslin warps, sized and ready for the loom, (being the first who sold cotton twist in that state, chiefly to Mr. Oldknow, the father of the muslin trade in our country). Some warps I sent to

Glasgow and Paisley. I also manufactured a few muslins myself. . . . William Radcliffe. *Origin of the New System of Manufacture, commonly called Power-Loom Weaving*, Stockport, 1828, 9–10

In Scotland several landowners participated in textile ventures during the early stages of the Industrial Revolution.
Their activities—and those of other entrepreneurs—were reported by parish ministers in *The Statistical Account of Scotland*
(Edinburgh, 21 vols, 1791–9), edited by Sir John Sinclair, 1st
baronet of Ulbster (1754–1835). In the first paragraph below the
Rev John Gordon, minister of Sorn, and in the subsequent extracts the Rev Robert Steven, describe the creation of the celebrated Catrine (Ayrshire) cotton mills by Claud Alexander (d
1809), in partnership with David Dale. Alexander had made a
fortune in India before buying the Ballochmyle estate in 1786. A
renowned agricultural improver, he was also a successful industrialist; but in 1801 the Catrine venture was sold to James
Finlay.

---

30 In the present times, the most distinguished improver,
beyond dispute, is Claude Alexander, Esq.; of Ballochmyle.
The greatest part of his property, indeed, and of course the
principal scene of his improvements, lies in the parish of
Mauchline. . . . In this parish, beside highly improving his
landed property, he has built the cotton-mills and village of
Catrine, which have infused new life and activity into this part
of the country. These various operations, he himself superin-
tends with unwearied attention and activity. . . .

Catrine is entirely a new creation, and owes its existence to
the flourishing state of the cotton manufacture in Great Britain.
In the year 1787, Mr. Alexander of Ballochmyle, the proprietor of the village in partnership with the patriotic Mr. Dale
of Glasgow, built a cotton-twist mill . . . with a fall of water,
from the dam-head to where it returns again to the river, of 46
feet. A jeanie factory and a corn-mill are drove by the same
fall. It is likewise proposed to erect a waulk or fulling mill on

H

this stream of water. The twist-mill consists of 5 square stories, besides garrets; and contains 5240 spindles, which are all going at present (December 1796). Three hundred and one persons, old and young, are just now employed, in carding, roving, and in spinning, with an overseer and two clerks: Clock-makers, smiths, mill-wrights, and other mechanics, amount to 15 more. The women, who pick cotton in their own houses, are at present 226. In all, belonging to the twist-mill, by last return, 445. Of these, 118 are under 12 years of age; 128 are between 12 and 20; and 200 are above 20 years of age. The total amount of wages paid from October 30. 1795, to October 28. 1796 is L.3193 Sterling; and, as far as can be ascertained, the average quantity of cotton spun weekly is 2660 libs. In the year 1790, the same company built a jeanie factory, which contains 76 jeanies. The carding, roving, &c. are performed by the tail-water of the twist-mill. Here 200 persons, including an over-seer, two clerks, and mechanics, find constant employment, besides 55 women who pick cotton in their own houses. Forty-three are under 12 years of age; 72 from 12 to 20; and the rest are above 20 years of age. The wages *per* week are about L.80 Sterling.

Children are not admitted into the work under 9 years old; and they all lodge with their parents or friends. It is but justice to add, that both old and young enjoy uniformly good health. . . .

. . . Weaving is only in its infancy here; however, a hundred looms are erected, but they are seldom all occupied at the same time. At present 91 are at work, and are chiefly employed by the cotton manufacturers in Glasgow and Paisley. The yarn spun here is sent to Glasgow weekly by the Company's carrier. Sir John Sinclair (ed). *The Statistical Account of Scotland*, XX, Edinburgh, 1798, 165, 176–7, 178

_____

Robert Owen (1771–1858), industrialist, humanitarian, eccentric, egoist, pioneer of trade union organisation and co-operation, and verbose propagandist, was scarcely a representa-tive example of the nineteenth-century employers. But in the following extract from his autobiography he shows the means by which a youth of humble background could become a man of some importance in the late eighteenth century. Owen's later career developed from his appointment as manager of the Manchester mill of Peter Drinkwater (d 1801) in 1792, manager of the Chorlton Twist Company in 1795, and manager and partner in the New Lanark Mills in 1797. His progress was considerably aided by his marriage, in 1799, to Caroline Dale, daughter of the founder of New Lanark, David Dale (1739–1806).

---

31 As it appears in the family great Bible, I was born in Newtown, Montgomeryshire, North Wales, on the 14th of May, 1771, and was baptised on the 12th of June following.

My father was Robert Owen. He was born in Welsh Pool, and was brought up to be a saddler, and probably an ironmonger also, as these two trades were at that period often united in the small towns on the borders of Wales. He married into the family of Williams, a numerous family, who were in my childhood among the most respectable farmers around Newtown.

. . . My father had written respecting me to his friend, a Mr. Heptinstall, of No. 6 Ludgate Hill, who was a large dealer in lace foreign and British; and Mr. Moore had written in my favor to Mr. Tilsley, of No. 100 Newgate Street, who then kept what was deemed a large draper's shop. This was in 1781. I think I had been on this visit to my brother nearly six weeks, when Mr. Heptinstall procured me a situation with a Mr. James McGuffog, of whom he spoke highly as carrying on a large business for a provincial town, in Stamford, Lincolnshire. The terms offered to me were for three years—the first without pay, the second with a salary of eight pounds, and the third with ten pounds, and with board, lodging, and washing, in the house. These terms I accepted, and being well found with clothes to serve me more than a year, I from that period, ten years of age, maintained myself without ever applying to my parents for any additional aid.

... After my three years had expired, Mr. McGuffog wished me to remain with him, and to continue as an assistant for a year longer ... [but] my wishes were for the attainment of more knowledge and an enlarged field of action. ...

... Having been so long absent from my relations and friends I was glad to spend some months with my brother William.

... After some time of this relaxation from business it was necessary for me to seek for a new situation, and through Mr. McGuffog's recommendation I procured one with Messrs. Flint and Palmer, an old established house on old London Bridge, Borough side, overlooking the Thames. It was a house established, and I believe the first, to sell at a small profit for ready money only. ...

... This hurried work and slavery of every day in the week appeared to me more than my constitution could support for a continuance, and before the spring trade had terminated I had applied to my friend to look out for another situation for me. ...

... On leaving Messrs. Flint and Palmer's, I went to reside with Mr. Satterfield in Manchester. His establishment was then the first in his line in the retail department, but not much to boast of as a wholesale warehouse. It was upon the whole pretty well managed. ...

Our living was good, our treatment kind, and ... I therefore soon became reconciled to the change which my friend had made for me, and with forty pounds a year, over my board, lodging, and washing, I deemed myself overflowing with wealth, having more than my temperate habits required ... I thus continued until I was eighteen years of age. Among other articles which we sold were wires for the foundation or frame of ladies' bonnets. The manufacturer of these wire bonnet-frames was a mechanic with some small inventive powers and a very active mind. When he brought his weekly supply of wire frames, I had to receive them from him, and he began to tell me about great and extraordinary discoveries that were begin-ning to be introduced into Manchester for spinning cotton by new and curious machinery. He said he was endeavouring to see and to get a knowledge of them, and that if he could succeed he could make a very good business of it. This kind of conversation was frequently renewed by the wire manufacturer, whose name was Jones. At length he told me he had succeeded in seeing these machines at work, and he was sure he could make them and work them. He had however no capital, and he could not begin without some. He said that with one hundred pounds he could commence and soon accumulate capital sufficient to proceed; and he ended by saying that if I would advance one hundred pounds, I should have one half of the great profits that were to result if I would join him in partnership. He made me believe that he had obtained a great secret, and that if assisted as he stated, he could soon make a good business. I wrote to my brother William in London, to ask him if he could conveniently advance me the sum required, and he immediately sent me the hundred pounds. . . . During the time between my giving notice and finally leaving Mr. Satterfield's establishment, Jones and I had agreed with a builder that he should erect and let to us a large machine workshop, with rooms also for some cotton spinners, and the building was finished by the time I left Mr. Satterfield. We had shortly about forty men at work to make machines, and we obtained wood, iron, and brass, for their construction, upon credit.

I soon found however that Jones was a mere working mechanic, without any idea how to manage workmen, or how to conduct business on the scale on which he had commenced.

I had not the slightest knowledge of this new machinery—had never seen it at work. I was totally ignorant of what was required; but as there were so many men engaged to work for us, I knew that their wages must be paid, and that if they were not well looked after, our business must soon cease and end in our ruin. . . . We made what are technically called "mules" for spinning cotton, sold them, and appeared to be carrying on a good business; while, having discovered the want of business capacity in my partner, I proceeded with fear and trembling.

. . . When I separated from Jones and the machine making business, I took a large newly erected building, or factory, as such places were then beginning to be called. It was situated in Ancoats Lane. I rented it from a builder of the name of Woodruff, with whom I afterwards went to board and lodge. From Jones and his new partner I received *three* out of *six* mule machines which were promised, with the reel and making up machine; and with this stock I commenced business for myself in a small part of one of the large rooms in this large building.

The machines were set to work, and I engaged three men to work them—that is, to spin cotton yarn or thread upon them from a previous preparation called rovings. . . .

. . . I had no machinery to make rovings, and was obliged to purchase them,—they were the half made materials to be spun into thread. I had become acquainted with two young industrious Scotchmen, of the names of McConnell and Kennedy, who had commenced about the same time as myself to make cotton machinery upon a small scale, and they had now proceeded so far as to make some of the machinery for preparing the cotton for the mule spinning machinery so far as to enable them to make the rovings, which they sold in that state to the spinners at a good profit. . . .

Such was the commencement of Messrs. McConnell and Kennedy's successful career as cotton spinners,—such the foundation of those palace-like buildings which were afterwards erected by this firm,—of the princely fortunes which they made by them, and of my own proceedings in Manchester and in New Lanark in Scotland. *They* could then only make the *rovings*, without finishing the thread; and I could only *finish* the thread, without being competent to make the *rovings*.

These are the kind of circumstances which, without our knowledge or control, from small beginnings produce very different results to any anticipated by us when we commence. Robert Owen. *The Life of Robert Owen. Written by Himself. With Selections from his Writings and Correspondence*, 1857, I, 1, 12, 17–26

John Heathcoat (1783–1861), a Derbyshire grazier's son, came of yeoman stock. Brought up in Derbyshire and Leicestershire, he served apprenticeships with local stockingers and frame-smiths and about 1800 became a journeyman frame-smith in Nottingham. Backed by a Derby solicitor, W. J. Lockett, Heathcoat bought out his master in 1804. His bobbin-net machines of 1808 and 1809 revolutionised lace manufacture, and he set up business at Loughborough. When his factory was ruined by Luddites in 1816, he moved to Tiverton in Devonshire, adding a French establishment in the 1820s. The inventor became a prosperous capitalist, a Whig MP, a landowner and founder of the Heathcoat-Amory dynasty, later a particularly enlightened line of industrialists.

32　The bobbin-net, or Nottingham lace manufacture, like that of muslin, could have had no existence in England, but from Crompton's invention, the mule, which spins yarn suitable for that delicate fabric. For this manufacture the best quality of cotton is used, spun into the finest yarn, and twisted into thread by the doubling frame. The application of the stocking frame to the making of lace, was first thought of and tried by a framwork knitter of Nottingham, named Hammond, about the year 1768—that era of great inventions. It was not, however, rendered completely successful till Mr. John Heathcoat, M.P. for Tiverton, made an important alteration and improvement in the frame, for which he obtained a patent in 1809. Mr. Heathcoat began life in humble circumstances at Nottingham, and made his fortune by this happy invention; and, being at once a man of talent and of business, he now fills the honourable station of member of parliament for Tiverton. He removed to the latter place soon after he had obtained his patent, owing to the riotous attacks made on his lace-frames at Nottingham. . . . On the expiration of Mr. Heathcoat's patent, in 1823, other improvements followed in rapid succession; and such was the perfection attained in the manufacture, and so surprisingly cheap, as well as beautiful, was the net produced, that this manufacture has nearly destroyed the old manufacture of net by hand upon the pillow in England, Belgium, and France. Edward Baines. *History of the Cotton Manufacture in Great Britain*, 1835, 340–1

Benjamin Gott (1762–1840) was the great pioneer of the factory system in Yorkshire's woollen industry. The son of a civil engineer, he was educated at Bingley Grammar School and in 1780 was apprenticed to Messrs Wormald and Fountaine, a prominent woollen merchant house at Leeds. He became the junior partner in the firm in 1785, increasing his stake on the deaths of John Wormald and Joseph Fountaine in 1786 and 1790. From 1790 to 1816 the Gotts and the Wormalds maintained the partnership. Unlike most Leeds merchants, they entered manufacturing industry, and in 1792 Gott built his great Bean Ing mills at Leeds. A Tory and a Churchman, he was Mayor of Leeds in 1799, a substantial contributor to Conservative and Anglican causes and an enlightened employer. The following transcriptions of Gott's partnership arrangements were made by Dr R. Offor and were originally published in W. B. Crump. *The Leeds Woollen Industry*, 1780–1820, Leeds, 1931, 194–5, 231–2. They are quoted by kind permission of the Thoresby Society. Gott's papers are now lodged in the Brotherton Library at Leeds University.

33 The Heads or Instructions for Articles of Copartnership between John Wormald of Leeds Esq[r] Joseph Fountaine of the same place Esq[r] and Benjamin Gott of the same place Merch[t] as follow:

First. The said John Wormald and Joseph Fountaine from the great confidence they have in the Integrity Honesty and Abilities of the said Benjamin Gott have Agreed to take and enter into Copartnership with him for the Term of Five Years commencing from the first day of January last, in the Trade or buisiness of Cloth Merchants which J.W. & J.F. now follow such Trade to be carried on and managed under the firm of Wormald Fountaine & Co.

2nd That Stock Cloth Debts (exclusive of bad Debts) and other Effects in Trade belonging to J.W. & J.F., which upon an Account and Valuation made upon the 1st January last, amounted to the Sum of £36,600 shall be taken as the Capital Advanced into the Trade by Messrs W. & F., Viz., £18,300 by J.W. and £18,300 by J.F., and that Benjn Gott shall advance into the Trade the sum of £3,660, which several Sums making together the Sum of 40,260£ Agreed to be the Capital Stock in Trade of the Copartners and to be used in the Trade for the best Advantage of all the parties according to their respective Interests therein.

3rd That all such Sums of Money as the Copartners now or shall have in the Trade over and above the respective Capitals aforesaid, shall be paid an Interest for at the Rate of £4. 10s. per Centum pr Annum.

4th That the Trade shall be carried on in and upon the premises belonging to J.W. where such Trade is now Managed and for which J.W. shall receive the sum of £60 as a Rent for the same.

5th That J.W. shall at any time during the said Term without any Gratuity or Apprentice Fee, take as an Apprentice or Apprentices any of his Sons to be initiated or instructed in the said Trade he the said J.W. at his own Expence providing for such Sons all necessaries.

6th That each of them J.W. & J.F. and each of their Executors and Administrators shall during the continuance and at the End of the copartnership have the full right property and Interest in 5 Eleventh parts, and Benjn Gott shall have the full right property and Interest in the remaining 1 Eleventh part of the joint Stock and other matters and things belonging to the Copartnership which shall remain after Payment of all Debts due on Account of the Copartnership, and also the same proportionable parts of all Gains, profits and increase which shall accrue by the said Trade and likewise pay all Losses Costs Charges and Expences Rents and Damages in the same Proportions.

7th   The Stock Buyings Sellings and all other matters relating
to the Copartnership to be entered into proper and suitable
Books for that purpose to be kept in the Countinghouse. . . .

8th   All Securities for Money or Goods taken for any matter
relating the Copartnership and all Goods to be Sold out of the
joint Stock or Trade upon Trust shall be made in the Names of
J.W. & J.F. and Benjn Gott and for their Benefit in the Proportions mentioned. . . .

9th   That no Credit shall be given to any person or persons
whom any of the parties shall forewarn should not be Credited,
Nor any Apprentice taken during the Copartnership but with
the joint consent of all the parties, except such of the Sons of
J.W. as he shall think proper to take as aforesaid nor any Debt,
Referred or Compounded without the Consent of the others. . . .

10th   That Benjn Gott may on the first Monday in every
Month during the Copartnership take out of the Profits of the
joint Stock the sum of 12 £ in his particular uses. And that
J.W. & J.F. may take out of the joint Stock and Profits thereof
so much Money as shall bear a due proportion to the said sum
of 12 £ to be taken thereout by Benjn Gott as their respective
Capitals bear to the Capital of Benjn Gott for their particular
uses.

11th   That at the End of the Copartnership or at any time
Afterwards during such time as Benjn Gott shall be connected
with J.W. & J.F. or either of them or with any part of their
Families Benjn Gott shall and will agree to take into the share
of the Trade all or any of the sons of the said J.W. when and
as they shall arrive at Age qualified to take a share in such
buisiness, So that the taking into partnership of the Sons of
J.W. or any of them does in no wise lessen the Share & Interest
of the said Benjn Gott in the joint Trade—and for that purpose
Benjn Gott shall enter into and give a Bond in a sufficient penalty
for that purpose.

12th   That no Benefit of Survivorship should be had or taken. . . .

13th   That each of the parties will execute proper Articles of
Copartnership.

Articles of Copartnership between John Wormald, Joseph Fountaine and Benjamin Gott, 1 Jan 1785

Memorandum of an Agreement of four parts made the 9th day of January 1817 between BENJAMIN GOTT the Elder of the first part, B. GOTT & RICHARD WORMALD as Executors of HARRY WORMALD deceased of the second part, RICHARD WORMALD of the third part & JOHN GOTT Merchant of the fourth part.

Abstract

Whereas (a) Benjamin Gott, Harry Wormald, Richard Wormald & John Gott prior to 1st January 1815 carried on the business of Cloth Merchants & Manufacturers in Leeds and (b) from the said day they carried on the same business in Copartnership with Benjamin Gott the Younger deceased until the death of Harry Wormald on 7th June 1816, & (c) after his death the surviving Partners continued the business until 31st December last when it was dissolved by mutual consent; and whereas (d) Benjamin Gott the Younger hath since departed this Life intestate the several parties have agreed as follows.

That Benjamin Gott & John Gott shall have the Mill called Park Mill or Bean Ing Mill with the Engine, Machinery Utensils & so much of the Land near to it as was comprized in the original purchase from Mr. Woodcock & in the exchange with Mr. Wilson & also on the South side of the River so much as lies on to the East side of the Wellington Turnpike Road and also the Lease of Burley Mill & all the Machinery and Utensils therein; the land to be reckoned at the original cost & the Road on the South side of the River at the prime cost of the Land, and the Mills, Buildings, Machinery & Utensils to be taken at the price at which they were valued on 1st January 1815; other land & buildings purchased of Mr. Pottgeisser & Christopher Wilson Esq. . . . to be paid for at the purchase price. But as the Mills Buildings Machinery & Utensils are from wear and tear and from the depressed state of Trade of much less value than in the said valuation, the Executors of Harry

Wormald have agreed to abate £5000 from his share of the valuation of Park Mill, and £1000 for Burley Mill, and Richard Wormald has agreed to abate from his share £5000 for Park Mill & £1000 for Burley Mill.

That Richard Wormald & the Executors of Harry Wormald shall have in Equal shares the remainder of the Land at Park Mill or Bean Ing on both sides of the River Aire at such price as the Land cost, the amount to be carried to their respective Debit as so much of their Capital, & shall have free use of the Bridge over the River so long as it continues passible.

That the Road now set out on the West boundary from the River to the new Road shall be paid for by Messieurs Gott and the Executors & Richard Wormald in Equal Moieties & used by them & their Tenants.

That the settlement of Partnership Accounts of 1st January 1815 shall be the basis of the new settlement.

That the Remainder of the Stock & Utensils in Trade Book Debts shall be taken by B.G. & J.G. who shall pay as in the said Account after various deductions including one of 12½% on the value of the Goods & Book debts to cover the risque of bad Debts and the trouble & expence of disposing of the Stock & collecting the Debts, with an additional allowance of 2½% from the shares of R.W. & the Executors in the Stock & Book Debts if the abatement of 12½% is insufficient.

Interest at 5% to be paid half-yearly to the Executors & to R.W. on the Money which shall be due to them from the Concern until the principal is paid.

That their shares in the money arising from the Mill Buildings Land & Machinery at Park Mill or Bean Ing taken by B.G. & J.G. shall be secured on mortgage of the Premises for seven years from the 1st January; & that the remainder of the Money due from the Concern shall be paid to them in ten years & secured by the Bond of B.G. & J.G.

Witness the Hands of the said parties

Benjamin Gott

Benjamin Gott Executor of Harry Wormald

Witness.   Richard Wormald
Thos Everard   Richard Wormald Executor of Hy Wormald
        Upton   John Gott
            Agreement on Dissolution of Partnership, 9 Jan 1817

In the autumn of 1841 the 'Young England' Tory Lord John
Manners, later 7th Duke of Rutland (1818–1906), toured
Lancashire, being alternately impressed and horrified by what
he saw. Above all he enjoyed his visit to the Grant brothers—
the 'Cheerybles' of Charles Dickens' *Nicholas Nickleby* and
'most exquisite old men' to Manners. The benevolent Grants
were self-made men, the sons of a Scot who, ruined by the
American War, tramped to Lancashire for work. In the following letter to an unknown correspondent (published in W. Hume
Elliot, *The Story of the 'Cheeryble' Grants*, Manchester, 1906,
197–9), William Grant recalls his early career. After great
success, the Grants' concerns were in difficulties by 1839, but
the brothers hesitated to retire because of the risk of causing
unemployment.

---

34 . . . My father was a dealer in cattle, and lost his property
in the year 1783. He got a letter of introduction to Mr. Arkwright (the late Sir Richard) and came by way of Skipton and
Manchester, accompanied by me. As we passed along the old
road, we stopped for a short time on the Park estate to view the
valley. My father exclaimed, 'What a beautiful valley! May
God Almighty bless it!' It reminded me of Speyside, but the
Irwell is not so large as the river Spey.

I recollected that Messrs. Peel & Yates were then laying the
foundation of their printworks at Ramsbottom. We went forward to Manchester and called upon Mr. Arkwright, but he
had so many applications then he could not employ him. There
were then only Arkwright's mill, on a small scale, and Thacary's
mill in Manchester. There was a mill on the Irwell belonging
to Mr. Douglas, two belonging to Messrs. Peel and Yates, the
one at Radcliffe Bridge the other at Hinds; and these were the

only mills then in Lancashire. My father then applied to Mr. Dinwiddie, a Scotch gentleman, who knew him in his prosperity, and who was a printer and manufacturer at Hampson Mill, near Bury. He agreed to give my father employment, and placed my brother James and me in situations, where we had an opportunity of acquiring a knowledge both of manufacturing and printing; and offered me a partnership when I had finished my apprenticeship. I declined his offer, and commenced business for myself on a small scale, assisted by my brothers John, Daniel, and Charles, and removed to Bury, where I was very successful, and in the course of a few years I removed to Manchester, and commenced printing in partnership with my brothers. My brother Daniel commenced travelling through the North of England and almost to every market town in Scotland. In 1806 we purchased the print works belonging to Sir Robert Peel. . . . In 1812 we purchased Nuttall factory. . . .

In 1818 we purchased Springside, and in 1827 we purchased the Park estate, and erected a monument to commemorate my father's first visit to this valley, and on the very spot where he and I stood admiring the scenery below. . . .

We attribute much of our prosperity, under Divine Providence, to the good example and good counsel of our worthy parents. . . .

William Grant Letter, 17 May 1839

———

The Employers   At New Lanark Robert Owen (see p 114) earned a reputation as a humane though domineering employer. He organised every aspect of life in the little community living around his mills; one opponent was to report a worker's complaint that 'there were drills and exercises and that they were dancing together till they were more fatigued than if they were working'. But Owen's dictatorship was well-intentioned: he reduced hours and provided education. On the experience of New Lanark he based his (largely disastrous) involvement in factory reform, trade unions, various co-operative and socialist schemes, and utopian communities. While his visionary schemes and personal arrogance often infuriated colleagues, Owen's ideals of a future society, however impractical, were always humanitarian.

---

35 TO THE SUPERINTENDENTS OF MANUFACTORIES, AND TO THOSE INDIVIDUALS GENERALLY, WHO, BY GIVING EMPLOYMENT TO AN AGGREGATED POPULATION, MAY EASILY ADOPT THE MEANS TO FORM THE SENTIMENTS AND MANNERS OF SUCH A POPULATION.

Like you, I am a manufacturer for pecuniary profit. But having for many years acted on principles the reverse in many respects of those in which you have been instructed, and having found my procedure beneficial to others and to myself, even in a pecuniary point of view, I am anxious to explain such valuable principles, that you and those under your influence may equally partake of their advantages.

In two Essays, already published, I have developed some of these principles, and in the following pages you will find still more of them explained, with some detail of their application to practice under the peculiar local circumstances in which I took the direction of the New Lanark Mills and Establishment.

By those details you will find that from the commencement of my management I viewed the population, with the mechanism and every other part of the establishment, as a system composed of many parts, and which it was my duty and interest so to combine, as that every hand, as well as every spring, lever, and wheel, should effectually co-operate to produce the greatest pecuniary gain to the proprietors.

Many of you have long experienced in your manufacturing operations the advantages of substantial, well-contrived, and well-executed machinery.

Experience has also shown you the difference of the results between mechanism which is neat, clean, well-arranged, and always in a high state of repair; and that which is allowed to be dirty, in disorder, without the means of preventing unnecessary friction, and which therefore becomes, and works, much out of repair.

In the first case the whole economy and management are good; every operation proceeds with ease, order, and, success. In the last, the reverse must follow, and a scene be presented of counteraction, confusion, and dissatisfaction among all the agents and instruments interested or occupied in the general process, which cannot fail to create a great loss.

If, then, due care as to the state of your inanimate machines can produce such beneficial results, what may not be expected if you devote equal attention to your vital machines, which are far more wonderfully constructed?

When you shall acquire a right knowledge of these, of their curious mechanism, of their self-adjusting powers; when the proper main-spring shall be applied to their varied movements,—you will become conscious of their real value, and you will readily be induced to turn your thoughts more frequently from your inanimate to your living machines; you will discover that the latter may be easily trained and directed to procure a large increase of pecuniary gain, while you may also derive from them high and substantial gratification.

Will you then continue to expend large sums of money to procure the best devised mechanism of wood, brass, or iron; to retain it in perfect repair; to provide the best substance for the prevention of unnecessary friction, and to save it from falling into premature decay?—Will you also devote years of intense application to understand the connection of the various parts of these lifeless machines, to improve their effective powers, and to calculate with mathematical precision all their minute and combined movements?—And when in these transactions you estimate time by minutes, and the money expended for the chance of increased gain by fractions, will you not afford some of your attention to consider whether a portion of your time and capital would not be more advantageously applied to improve your living machines? From experience which cannot deceive me, I venture to assure you, that your time and money so applied, if directed by a true knowledge of the subject, would return you, not five, ten, or fifteen per cent. for your capital so expended, but often fifty, and in many cases a hundred per cent.

I have expended much time and capital upon improvements of the living machinery; and it will soon appear that the time and money so expended in the manufactory at New Lanark, even while such improvements are in progress only, and but half their beneficial effects attained, are now producing a return exceeding fifty per cent., and will shortly create profits equal to cent. per cent. on the original capital expended in them.

Indeed, after experience of the beneficial effects from due care and attention to the mechanical implements, it became easy to a reflecting mind to conclude at once, that at least equal advantages would arise from the application of similar care and attention to the living instruments. And when it was perceived that inanimate mechanism was greatly improved by being made firm and substantial; that it was the essence of economy to keep it neat, clean, regularly supplied with the best substance to prevent unnecessary friction, and by proper provision for the purpose to preserve it in good repair; it was natural to conclude that the more delicate, complex, living mechanism, would be equally improved by being trained to strength and activity; and that it would also prove true economy to keep it neat and clean; to treat it with kindness, that its mental movements might not experience too much irritating friction; to endeavour by every means to make it more perfect; to supply it regularly with a sufficient quantity of wholesome food and other necessaries of life, that the body might be preserved in good working condition, and prevented from being out of repair, or falling prematurely to decay.

These anticipations are proved by experience to be just.

Since the general introduction of inanimate mechanism into British manufactories, man, with few exceptions, has been treated as a secondary and inferior machine; and far more

I

attention has been given to perfect the raw materials of wood and metals than those of body and mind. Give but due reflection to the subject, and you will find that man, even as an instrument for the creation of wealth, may be still greatly improved.

But, my friends, a far more interesting and gratifying consideration remains. Adopt the means which ere long shall be rendered obvious to every understanding, and you may not only partially improve those living instruments, but learn how to impart to them such excellence as shall make them infinitely surpass those of the present and all former times.

Here, then, is an object which truly deserves your attention; and, instead of devoting all your faculties to invent improved inanimate mechanism, let your thoughts be, at least in part, directed to discover how to combine the more excellent materials of body and mind, which, by a well devised experiment, will be found capable of progressive improvement.

Thus seeing with the clearness of noonday light, thus convinced with the certainty of conviction itself, let us not perpetuate the really unnecessary evils which our present practices inflict on this large proportion of our fellow-subjects. Should your pecuniary interests somewhat suffer by adopting the line of conduct now urged, many of you are so wealthy that the expense of founding and continuing at your respective establishments the institutions necessary to improve your animate machines would not be felt. But when you may have ocular demonstration, that, instead of any pecuniary loss, a well-directed attention to form the character and increase the comforts of those who are so entirely at your mercy, will essentially add to your gains, prosperity, and happiness, no reasons, except those founded on ignorance of your self-interest, can in future prevent you from bestowing your chief care on the living machines which you employ. And by so doing you will prevent an accumulation of human misery, of which it is now difficult to form an adequate conception.

That you may be convinced of this most valuable truth,

which due reflection will show you is founded on the evidence of unerring facts, is the sincere wish of

THE AUTHOR.

Robert Owen. Address prefacing the Third Essay of *A New View of Society; or, Essays on the Principle of the Formation of the Human Character, and The Application of the Principle to Practice,* 1813

John Wood (1793–1871), the son of a prosperous comb and lantern manufacturer, entered the Bradford worsted industry as an apprentice, setting up his own spinning and combing business in 1812. Helped by paternal capital, local development, and personal acumen, by the early 1830s he was the largest worsted employer, with some 3,000 workers. With several other early Bradford worsted masters, he was a Tory, Evangelical Anglican, and supporter of factory legislation. He provided a factory school for 500 children in 1832, introduced a ten-hour day in 1833, largely financed the factory reformers, and was a major benefactor of local charities, schools, and churches. Wood inherited £500,000 and augmented the family fortune. From the mid-1830s he gradually retired from the business, leaving management to his half-cousin William Walker (1803–67), another Tory Churchman and reformer (who is unfairly described below). When Wood left the business in 1854 he was a Hampshire squire; and in the 1860s Walker & Company declined. Few employers received such eulogies from workmen as Wood was given in the following piece of John Clark's manuscript—part transcript and part commentary— which is now in Bradford City Library.

---

36 The "Penny Magazine" published by the Society for Useful Knowledge contains an article on Saturday, November 16th 1833, headed:

"A well conducted Factory.

(From a Correspondent)

The general tenor of the evidence, given before the Factory Commissioners goes to show that although there may be great abuses in many establishments in which children are employed, extensive factories may and do exist where the light spirits of youth are still buoyant and unbroken by undue labour and restraint, and where the industry of the young not only contributes to the increase of our national wealth, but also to their own advantage. In some factories they are not only usefully employed, but at the same time, are trained up in those habits of morality and good feeling which are most likely to ensure their own lasting happiness and make them valuable members of society. We have recently returned from visiting some factories and among the rest that of Mr. John Wood junr., a stuff manufacturer at Bradford in Yorkshire. We think it may do some good in two ways if we give a very slight sketch of what we there saw. Such an outline may serve to correct some of the prejudices which exist on the subject of factories amongst those who have never visited the seat of any great manufacturer; while those masters who look only to the accumulation of money, may take shame themselves when they find that the same object may be obtained without injury to the health and morals of children.

In the manufactory of Mr. Wood about 600 persons principally girls are employed. When we arrived it was the hour allotted for dinner and recreation and the young people were joyously sporting in the open yard of the factory, like children out of school. After witnessing for some time this scene of unrestrained freedom from toil, the period for renewed industry arrived, and we were ushered into the mill. This we found as clean as light, and as comfortable as a drawing room or rather as a series of drawing rooms, for there are several floors filled with machinery.

The children in resuming their work, had not lost their cheerful look, and set about their tasks in a manner which proved that they were anything but irksome to them. Seats are provided for the accommodation of the young folk, when they are not actually employed, which state of leisure very frequently occurs. The little workpeople seemed quite delighted to see their employer; their faces brightened up and their eyes sparkled as he came near and spoke to them; indeed he appeared to be more like a father among them, and an affectionate one too, than like a master; patting them on the head, chucking them under the chin, and addressing them according to their ages. There is always a surplus number of children in the mill in order that they may be sent by instalments to a school room on the premises, where they learn to knit and sew as well as to read and write. The reason given by their benevolent employer for having them taught knitting and needle-work shows how mindful he is of their future welfare. He said that when girls, who had been employed from an early age in a mill, were married, they made unprofitable wives, for not knowing how to perform the necessary parts of a wife's and mother's duties— they did not know how to employ themselves and consequently became idle gossips. A schoolmaster resides on the premises, and Mr. Wood allows other poor children, besides those employed in the mill to attend the school. A medical man is engaged to visit the factory weekly to examine into the general health of the children and gives more frequent attendance to those who are ill. With regard to the hours of work the Factory Bill recently will just make a difference of ten minutes a day. The children are expected to appear in clean clothes twice a week; Saturday is the worst day in the week in this respect, and on that day some of the young people are employed in cleaning the place. It happened to be on a Saturday we viewed the factory, and therefore not at the most favourable time; the young folk do not like visitors on that day, and there was in consequence some slight scruple at admitting us; but every one and every thing appeared to us nice and clean and in order, and we could not detect among the children any signs that the renewed cleanliness of the morrow was required.

We questioned the proprietor as to the morals of the older girls, when he assured us that they are perfectly good, and added that he was certain if any one among them was known to misconduct herself, the rest would immediately apply to him

to dismiss her from among them. Mr. Wood never found any
difficulty in training the children according to his wishes; at
first he had some trouble to induce the parents to co-operate
with him in his plans, but this obstacle to improvement is
entirely overcome.

Mr. Wood is a wool-sorter, and wool-comber, as well as a
spinner; and in those branches employs men of some skill, who
appeared to be very decent; not one did we see who bore the
marks of vice and drunkeness about him. They seemed to be
on the best terms with their employer. Whenever he entered
any room where they were at work, he addressed them with
"Good morning, how do you all do", which was answered by
an inquiry about his health, and in addition in one or two cases
of "It is some days since we have seen you Sir". In fact all
seemed glad to see him, as if it were felt and fully recognized
that his was the grateful task to watch over them and promote
their general good and that only one common interest existed
between them.

Happy is it for society when the employer and the employed
have such a connexion of goodwill between them, and most
happy are those who can combine with their own gainful pur-
suits the gratification which always accompanies warmhearted
and enlightened benevolence."

Mr. Wood had deeply lamented the long hours children in
mills were obliged to toil and he commenced working 10 hours
a day and letting the children go at 6 instead of 8 o'clock
during the dark and dreary winter months, he commenced on
Monday, Nov. 25th 1833. The day following the Parents of the
children called a Public Meeting to return him thanks and to
call the attention of other Masters to follow so laudable and
praiseworthy an example.

The meeting agreed that a deputation should wait upon Mr.
Wood to "return him sincere and heartfelt thanks for his
humane and considerate conduct in allowing his factory
workers to labour only 10 hours a day, during the winter
months, without reducing their wages."

Extract from the "Leeds Mercury" of Saturday, Nov. 1st 1834.
"The proprietors of factories have prodigious influence, which they may use either for good or evil. Humane and religious masters, by establishing regulations favourable to virtue, discountenancing vice and irregularity, may do more than ministers, parents, and friends, to bind the workpeople to a virtuous course. No master is bound to keep an immoral man in his employment; on the contrary for the sake of his other workpeople and from regard to his own property and interests, he is bound to dismiss that man.

But we should greatly prefer to see the workpeople allured and encouraged to virtue than merely deterred from vice. Let the masters attend to the comfort and health of their workmen, let them shew a kindly interest in their welfare, let them encourage their sick societies, Sunday Schools, week evening schools, libraries, etc. and they will gain a moral influence among the operatives, which may be turned to great account. There are several mills in Yorkshire and Lancashire, which we have seen with great delight, and which could not fail to give sincere pleasure to every sincere philanthropic observer. Amongst them we must say that the worsted mill of Mr. John Wood of Bradford stands pre-eminent for the admirable cleanliness, the perfect ventilation, the real comfort of the mill—the decency, the healthfulness and the happiness of the workpeople of both sexes, and of all ages, and the provision made by the benevolent owner for the education of the children, in a school maintained at his own expense, where both boys and girls are well taught, and the girls learn to knit and sew the very articles they will have to make when they become wives and mothers. Such a mill is a blessing, to the district in which it is situated, and an honour to the proprietors."

In June 1835 the elegant household furniture that decorated Horton House and Cavenby Lodge was put up to auction in the Exchange Buildings with a very large stock of Wine &c. belonging to John Wood Esqr., of some kinds of wine there were 3 *hogsheads*, of others many *pipes*, with an immense quantity of Bottled Port 8 & 10 years old. Most of the articles sold for more than their original cost.

Mr. Wood has taken William Walker as a *partner* in the concern, he is to be the managing partner, henceforth it will be designated *Wood's & Walker's.*

Mr. Wood is leaving Bradford & going to reside at *Theddon Grange Hants.* He will only pay a visit to Bradford about twice a year. If there be one man more than another whose withdrawal from the town will be severely felt & universally lamented & regretted it is Mr. John Wood whose charity & benevolence has endeared him to all around. The poor & the needy has lost a good friend, Christian societies and benevolent institutions have lost a munificent patron & his workpeople have lost one of the best & kindest of masters.

I am sorry to state that this Mr. Walker is far from being like Mr. Wood. He seems to be just the reverse, he is an unjust and tyranical man his actions mean & treats the workpeople with all the austerity & harshness of a despotic ruler; he excites the envy & increases the malice of the poor against him; his life has sometimes been placed in jeopardy & mobs has assembled & broke the lamps & windows of his own house. Oh that he would be wise & imitate him who has raised him from the dunghill & placed him on the house tops, where if care is not taken, great will be the fall of that Man.

"Leeds Times" August 13th 1836.

"Pro Bono Publico.—John Wood Esqr. of Bradford with his wonted liberality is erecting an excellent and expensive clock at his works, Goodmansend, which will strike quarterly and the hours, having three grand sizeable and tuneable bells for the purpose. This will be of great utility, to people in that part of the town, to whom the present clocks of the Church and Piece Hall are nearly if not altogether useless."

. . . In Octr. 1836 Mr. Wood accompanied with Lord Ashley came to Bradford, but prior to this a Manchester Paper relates as follows:

"We have great pleasure in announcing that the Rt. Hon.

Lord Ashley, accompanied by Mr. John Wood of Bradford and
Mr. Jowett of London, visited Macclesfield and inspected
several silk & other factories. His Lordship now and then
stumbled over a few crippled and deformed persons from long
hours of factory labour. They visited Stockport. His Lordship
visited several residences of the workpeople in the London
Road and Little Ireland and also in Blossom St. he visited
several residences of factory workers, and expressed his con-
victions to be still stronger in favour of a ten hour bill, that the
people might have more time to be clean and become frugal.

His Lordship visited the Railway, and minutely inquired
how the accident had occurred to Mr. Huskisson. His Lordship's sister, the Honourable Lady Charlotte was on the Railway when Mr. Huskisson was killed. On Friday they went to
Bury and from thence to Todmorden to visit Mr. John Fielden,
M.P. for Oldham. From thence they proceeded to Bradford in
Yorkshire, where Mr. John Wood was about to lay the first
stone of a new church in Manchester Road, to be called St.
James's"—the interesting ceremonial of which I have given an
account elsewhere, and of which *Lord Ashley* was an eye
witness. . . .

Mr. Wood is about 5ft. 10 inches high, has black hair,
pleasant and cheerful appearance and altogether the look of
the gentlemen. He has had issue two daughters, by his present
wife. My father was in his employ 15 years. In his sickness he
visited him & paid the greatest attention towards him & he
said this to the honour of my father after his visit "that *him* &
his *house* did honour to his works." Mr. Wood & I have been on
the most friendly terms, I have visited & dined with [him]
several times, he has made me presents of money & books. . . .
I esteem the present as a great prize not from the value but on
account of the noble Donor. Throughout his life up to the
present time 1840 it has always been characterized and distinguished for benevolence, piety & usefulness. May his life be
long spared, his imitators many, his troubles few, his pleasures
great, his path smooth & his death happy when called away.

Mr. Wood is worth more than a Million of money.   John
Clark. 'History & Annals of Bradford Yorkshire, or a Family
Book of Refference of the Most Important Events that have
Transpired there in Ancient & Modern Times, by John Clark,
a Native of that Place', 1840, 182–92

PART THREE

The Factory System Established

Following the success of the early factory pioneers, the new industrial system spread rapidly. There where two cotton mills in the Manchester area in 1782 and ninety-nine in 1830, nineteen in Scotland in 1787 and 125 in 1834. By 1835 there were 1,262 cotton mills in the United Kingdom, 683 of them in Lancashire. In the more slowly developing woollen industry 129 mills were in operation by 1833. By 1837 the Factory Inspectors were dealing with 4,283 mills affected by the Factory Act of 1833. As the mills and factories spread over the industrial areas, domestic work declined and some old textile districts, far removed from the coal areas, lost much of their industry. In general, cotton production came to be centred mainly in Lancashire and the Glasgow region, while the woollen industry was most strongly concentrated in the West Riding, with Bradford and Halifax dominating the worsted section. The 'dark, satanic mills' of the early stages of the Industrial Revolution were followed by buildings which (wrote William Carpenter in 1844) 'were much more comfortable and healthy for the workpeople'. But the revolution in the textile industries inevitably produced social changes and disturbances, as well as an important, successful middle class. In 1806 the cotton industry's 90,000 factory workers were overbalanced by 184,000 handloom weavers; by 1820 the totals were 126,000 and 240,000, in 1850 331,000 and

43,000, and in 1862 452,000 and 3,000. Such figures give one indication of the extent and pace of change.

The Factory System   Dr Andrew Ure (1778–1857) was a prominent and determined upholder of the virtues of the factory system. A scientist by training, he was Professor of Chemistry and Natural Philosophy in Anderson's College, Glasgow (now the University of Strathclyde) from 1804 to 1830. His knowledge of contemporary industry was apparently based on a short tour of the English cotton districts in 1833, and he naïvely accepted the views of ultra-liberal employers. From 1830 he worked in London as a consultant and chemist; and his boundless self-confidence led him to become the classic apologist for the factory system. 'The Pindar of Manufactures', the great admirer of the discipline and order of factory organisation, Ure was almost inevitably mocked by socialists such as Marx.

---

37   This island is pre-eminent among civilized nations for the prodigious development of its factory wealth, and has been therefore long viewed with a jealous admiration by foreign powers. This very pre-eminence, however, has been contemplated in a very different light by many influential members of our own community, and has been even denounced by them as the certain origin of innumerable evils to the people, and of revolutionary convulsions to the state. If the affairs of the kingdom be wisely administered, I believe such allegations and fears will prove to be groundless, and to proceed more from the envy of one ancient and powerful order of the commonwealth, towards another suddenly grown into political importance, than from the nature of things.

In the recent discussions concerning our factories, no circumstance is so deserving of remark, as the gross ignorance evinced by our leading legislators and economists,—gentlemen well informed in other respects,—relative to the nature of those stupendous manufactures which have so long provided the rulers of the kingdom with the resources of war, and a great body of the people with comfortable subsistence; which have, in fact, made this island the arbiter of many nations, and the benefactor of the globe itself.* Till this ignorance be dispelled, no sound legislation need be expected on manufacturing subjects. . . .

The blessings which physico-mechanical science has bestowed on society, and the means it has still in store for ameliorating the lot of mankind, has been too little dwelt upon; while, on the other hand, it has been accused of lending itself to the rich capitalists as an instrument for harassing the poor, and of exacting from the operative an accelerated rate of work. It has been said, for example, that the steam-engine now drives the power-looms with such velocity as to urge on their attendant weavers at the same rapid pace; but that the hand-weaver, not being subjected to this restless agent, can throw his shuttle and move his treddles at his convenience. There is, however, this difference in the two cases, that in the factory, every member of the loom is so adjusted, that the driving force leaves the attendant nearly nothing at all to do, certainly no muscular fatigue to sustain, while it procures for him good, unfailing wages, besides a healthy workshop *gratis*: whereas the non-factory weaver, having everything to execute by muscular exertion, finds the labour irksome, makes in consequence innumerable short pauses, separately of little account, but great when added together; earns therefore proportionaly low wages, while he loses his health by poor diet and the dampness of his hovel. Dr. Carbutt of Manchester says, "With regard to Sir Robert Peel's assertion a few evenings ago, that the hand-loom weavers are mostly small farmers, nothing can be a greater mistake; they live, or rather they just keep life together, in the most miserable manner, in the cellars and garrets of the town,

* Even the eminent statesman lately selected by his Sovereign to wield the destinies of this commercial empire—Sir Robert Peel, who derives his family consequence from the cotton trade, seems to be but little conversant with its nature and condition. . . .

working sixteen or eighteen hours for the merest pittance."*

The constant aim and effect of scientific improvement in manufactures are philanthropic, as to tend to relieve the workmen either from niceties of adjustment which exhaust his mind and fatigue his eyes, or from painful repetition of efforts which distort or wear out his frame. . . .

The term *Factory System*, in technology, designates the combined operation of many orders of work-people, adult and young, in tending with assiduous skill a series of productive machines continuously impelled by a central power. This definition includes such organizations as cotton-mills, flax-mills, silk-mills, woollen-mills, and certain engineering works; but it excludes those in which the mechanisms do not form a connected series, nor are dependent on one prime mover. Of the latter class, examples occur in iron-works, dye-works, soap-works, brass-foundries, &c. Some authors, indeed, have comprehended under the title *factory*, all extensive establishments wherein a number of people co-operate towards a common purpose of art; and would therefore rank breweries, distilleries, as well as the workshops of carpenters, turners, coopers, &c., under the factory system. But I conceive that this title, in its strictest sense, involves the idea of a vast automaton, composed of various mechanical and intellectual organs, acting in uninterrupted concert for the production of a common object, all of them being subordinated to a self-regulated moving force. If the marshalling of human beings in systematic order for the execution of any technical enterprise were allowed to constitute a factory, this term might embrace every department of civil and military engineering,—a latitude of application quite inadmissible. . . .

. . . In my recent tour, continued during several months, through the manufacturing districts, I have seen tens of thousands of old, young, and middle-aged of both sexes, many of them too feeble to get their daily bread by any of the former

* Letter of 3rd of May, 1833, to Dr. Hawkins in his Medical Report, Factory Commission, p. 382.

modes of industry, earning abundant food, raiment, and domestic accommodation, without perspiring at a single pore, screened meanwhile from the summer's sun and the winter's frost, in apartments more airy and salubrious than those of the metropolis in which our legislative and fashionable aristocracies assemble. In those spacious halls the benignant power of steam summons around him his myriads of willing menials, and assigns to each the regulated task, substituting for painful muscular effort on their part, the energies of his own gigantic arm, and demanding in return only attention and dexterity to correct such little aberrations as casually occur in his work-manship. The gentle docility of this moving force qualifies it for impelling the tiny bobbins of the lace-machine with a precision and speed inimitable by the most dexterous hands, directed by the sharpest eyes. Hence, under its auspices, and in obedience to Arkwright's polity, magnificent edifices, sur-passing far in number, value, usefulness, and ingenuity of con-struction, the boasted monuments of Asiatic, Egyptian, and Roman despotism, have, within the short period of fifty years, risen up in this kingdom, to show to what extent capital, industry, and science may augment the resources of a state, while they meliorate the condition of its citizens. Such is the factory system, replete with prodigies in mechanics and political economy, which promises in its future growth to become the great minister of civilization to the terraqueous globe, enabling this country, as its heart, to diffuse along with its commerce the life-blood of science and religion to myriads of people still lying "in the region and shadow of death". Andrew Ure. *The Philosophy of Manufactures: or, An Exposition of the Scientific, Moral, and Commercial Economy of the Factory System of Great Britain*, 1835, 5–8, 13–14, 17–19

_____

The Lancashire Cotton Industry   The most rapidly ex-panding textile industry, cotton, was the first 'trade' in the world to develop a full-scale factory system and to experience the consequent social dislocations. The benevolent Dr Aikin appreciated the benefits of the new machines of the late eighteenth century, but also drew public attenion to some of the disadvantages of the developing industry. He wrote during a transitional stage, when cotton spinning was being concentrated in mainly water-powered mills. Several other medical men and clergymen agreed with his assessment of the social, moral, and physical results of long factory hours. In 1796 the pioneer Manchester 'Board of Health', under Dr Thomas Perceval (1740–1804) pronounced that 'large factories were generally injurious to the constitution of those employed in them'. Thus a movement of protest was in gestation through the time of the factory system's major development.

---

38 . . . No exertions of the masters or workmen could have answered the demands of trade without the introduction of *spinning machines*.

These were first used by the country people on a confined scale, twelve spindles being thought a great matter; while the awkward posture required to spin on them was discouraging to grown up people, who saw with surprise children from nine to twelve years of age manage them with dexterity, whereby plenty was brought into families formerly overburthened with children, and the poor weavers were delivered from the bondage in which they had lain from the insolence of spinners. . . .

The invention and improvements of machines to shorten labour, has had a surprising influence to extend our trade, and also to call in hands from all parts, especially children for the cotton mills. It is the wise plan of Providence, that in this life there should be no good without its attendant inconvenience. There are many which are too obvious in these cotton mills, and similar factories, which counteract that increase of population usually consequent on the improved facility of labour. In these, children of very tender age are employed; many of them collected from the workhouses in London and Westminster, and transported in crowds, as apprentices to masters resident many hundred miles distant, where they serve unknown, unprotected, and forgotten by those to whose care nature or the laws had consigned them. These children are usually too long confined to work in close rooms, often during the whole night; the air they breathe from the oil, &c., employed in the machinery, and other circumstances, is injurious; little regard is paid to their cleanliness, and frequent changes from a warm and dense to a cold and thin atmosphere, are predisposing causes to sickness and disability, and particularly to the epidemic fever which so generally is to be met with in these factories. It is also much to be questioned, if society does not receive detriment from the manner in which children are thus employed during their early years. They are not generally strong to labour, or capable of pursuing any other branch of business, when the term of their apprenticeship expires. The females are wholly uninstructed in sewing, knitting, and other domestic affairs, requisite to make them notable and frugal wives and mothers. This is a very great misfortune to them and the public, as is sadly proved by a comparison of the families of labourers in husbandry, and those of manufacturers in general. In the former we meet with neatness, cleanliness, and comfort; in the latter with filth, rags, and poverty; although their wages may be nearly double to those of the husbandman. It must be added, that the want of early religious instruction and example, and the numerous and indiscriminate association in these buildings, are very unfavourable to their future conduct in life. To mention these grievances, is to point out their remedies; and in many factories they have been adopted with true benevolence and much success. But in all cases "The public have a right to see that its members are not wantonly injured, or carelessly lost".

... Since the opposition of the populace to the use of machines for shortening labour has been quelled by convincing them of their utility, spinning factories have been erected throughout all the surrounding country [near Bolton], especially where water is plentiful. The streams near Bolton are too near their

K

sources to furnish the water that large works require; there are few, therefore, in its neighbourhood of the larger kind, though several of the smaller. Much water is also occupied by the bleachers, who have extensive crofts here. . . . The want of water in this district is made up by the ingenious invention of the machines called mules, or hall-in-the-wood wheels, from an old hall in the neighbourhood seated in a most romantic situation, in part of which the inventor resided. This machine admits of a great number of spindles; the greatest yet known is 304. Had the inventor sought a patent, he might probably have acquired a large fortune; but some gentlemen in Manchester purchased the invention for 100 *l* and made it public.

. . . Manchester on [Tuesdays, Thursdays and Saturdays] is crowded with traders and makers of cotton goods from the country round, on the Tuesday particularly. The goods are not exposed in a public hall as the Yorkshire cloths are; their vast quantity and variety would not admit of such a mode. The expenses of importing the raw materials, and the extent of the trade, have enabled men of some property to step in between the weaver and merchant, and to obtain a profit upon the materials and goods in every stage of their progress.

. . . The extensiveness of the whole concern [Robert Peel's 'very capital manufacturing and printing works'] is such as to find constant employ for most of the inhabitants of Bury and its neighbourhood, of both sexes and all ages, and notwithstanding their great number, they have never wanted work in the most unfavourable times. The peculiar healthiness of the people employed may be imputed partly to the judicious and humane regulations put in practice by Mr. Peel, and partly to the salubrity of the air and climate.

. . . The cotton trade introduced [in Dukinfield], while it affords employment to all ages, has debilitated the constitutions and retarded the growth of many, and made an alarming increase in the mortality. The effect is greatly to be attributed to the pernicious custom, so properly reprobated by Dr. Percival and other physicians, of making the children in the mills work by night and day, one set getting out of bed when another goes into the same, thus never allowing the rooms to be well ventilated. John Aikin. *A Description of the Country from thirty to forty Miles round Manchester*, 1795, 167, 219–20, 262–3, 268–9, 456

As has been seen, the spinning process was mechanised in the late eighteenth century, aided by water or steam power. The progress of the power-loom was much slower: in 1813 only about 2,000 were in use. But after the Napoleonic war ended in 1815 there were many improvements and many adoptions of powered weaving. In 1829 there were over 45,000 power-looms in operation in England and six years later 96,679. The consequences for the hand-weavers were increasingly disastrous. Richard Guest, writing during the period of rapid growth of power-loom factories, here gives an early description of the change.

39 ... Before the invention of the dressing frame, one weaver was required to each steam loom, at present a boy or girl, 14 or 15 years of age, can manage two steam looms, and with their help can weave three and a half times as much cloth as the best hand weaver. The best hand weavers seldom produce a piece of uniform evenness; indeed, it is next to impossible for them to do so, because a weaker or stronger blow with the lathe immediately alters the thickness of the cloth, and after an interruption of some hours, the most experienced weaver finds it difficult to recommence with a blow of precisely the same force as the one with which he left off. In steam looms, the lathe gives a steady, certain blow, and when once regulated by the engineer, moves with the greatest precision from the beginning to the end of the piece. Cloth made by these looms when seen by those manufacturers who employ hand weavers, at once excites admiration and a consciousness that their own workmen cannot equal it. The increasing number of steam looms is a certain proof of their superiority over the hand looms. In 1818, there were in Manchester, Stockport, Middleton, Hyde, Staley Bridge, and their vicinities, 14 factories, containing about 2,000 looms. In 1821, there were in the same neighbourhoods 32 factories, containing 5,732 looms. Since 1821, their number has still farther increased, and there are at present not less than 10,000 steam looms at work in Great Britain.

It is a curious circumstance, that, when the cotton manufacture was in its infancy, all the operations, from the dressing of the raw material to its being fully turned out in the state of cloth, were completed under the roof of the weaver's cottage. The course of improved manufacture which followed, was to spin the yarn in factories and to weave it in cottages. At the present time, when the manufacture has attained a mature growth, all the operations, with vastly increased means and more complex contrivances, are again performed in a single building. The weaver's cottage with its rude apparatus of peg warping, hand cards, hand wheels, and imperfect looms, was the steam loom factory in miniature. Those vast brick edifices in the vicinity of all the great manufacturing towns in the south of Lancashire, towering to the height of 70 or 80 feet, which strike the attention and excite the curiosity of the traveller, now perform labours which formerly employed whole villages. In the steam loom factories, the cotton is carded, roved, spun, and woven into cloth, and the same quantum of labour is now performed in one of these structures which formerly occupied the industry of an entire district.

A very good hand weaver, a man 25 or 30 years of age, will weave 2 pieces of nine-eighths shirting per week, each 24 yards long, and containing 105 shoots of weft in an inch, the reed of the cloth being a 44, Bolton count, and the warp and weft 40 hanks to the pound. A steam-loom weaver, 15 years of age, will in the same time weave 7 similar pieces. A steam loom factory containing 200 looms, with the assistance of 100 persons under 20 years of age, and of 25 men, will weave 700 pieces per week, of the length and quality before described. To manufacture 100 pieces per week by the hand, it would be necessary to employ at least 125 looms, because many of the weavers are females, and have cooking, washing, cleaning and various other duties to perform; others of them are children, and consequently unable to weave as much as the men. It requires a man of mature age and a very good weaver to weave 2 of the pieces in a week, and there is also an allowance to be made for sickness and other incidents. Thus, 875 hand looms would be required to produce the 700 pieces per week; and reckoning the weavers, with their children, and the aged and infirm belonging to them, at $2\frac{1}{2}$ to each loom, it may very safely be said, that the work done in a steam factory containing 200 looms, would, if done by hand weavers, find employment and support for a population of more than 2,000 persons. Richard Guest. *A Compendious History of the Cotton Manufacture*, 1823, 46–8

Samuel Bamford [see p 69] here describes some of the post-war Radical activity in the Lancashire cotton districts, which was widely copied by working people. Bamford was involved in the Hampden Clubs, reviving demands for a wider suffrage and opposing agricultural protection. Disillusionment with the bleak economic conditions of the Peace of 1815 led to 'food riots', renewed machine-wrecking, appeals to Parliament, minor insurrectionary movements, and the use of spies and 'repressive' legislation by the Government of Lord Liverpool. The climax was reached with the so-called 'Peterloo Massacre' at Manchester in 1819, when overzealous Yeomanry killed eleven people while attempting to arrest the Radical orator Henry Hunt (1773–1835). Ministerial strength and improving economic conditions thereafter dampened proletarian militancy.

40 It is matter of history, that whilst the laurels were yet cool on the brows of our victorious soldiers on their second occupation of Paris, the elements of convulsion were at work amongst the masses of our labouring population; and that a series of disturbances commenced with the introduction of the Corn

Bill in 1815, and continued, with short intervals, until the close of the year 1816. In London and Westminster riots ensued, and were continued for several days, whilst the bill was discussed; at Bridport, there were riots on account of the high price of bread; at Biddeford there were similar disturbances to prevent the exportation of grain; at Bury, by the unemployed, to destroy machinery; at Ely, not suppressed without bloodshed; at Newcastle-on-Tyne, by colliers and others; at Glasgow, where blood was shed, on account of the soup kitchens; at Preston, by unemployed weavers; at Nottingham, by Luddites, who destroyed thirty frames; at Merthyr Tydville, on a reduction of wages; at Birmingham, by the unemployed; at Walsall, by the distressed; and December 7th, 1816, at Dundee, where owing to the high price of meal, upwards of one hundred shops were plundered. At this time the writings of William Cobbett suddenly became of great authority; they were read on nearly every cottage hearth in the manufacturing districts of South Lancashire, in those of Leicester, Derby, and Nottingham; also in many of the Scottish manufacturing towns. Their influence was speedily visible; he directed his readers to the true cause of their sufferings—misgovernment; and to its proper corrective—parliamentary reform. Riots soon became scarce, and from that time they have never obtained their ancient vogue with the labourers of this country.

Let us not descend to be unjust. Let us not withhold the homage, which, with all the faults of William Cobbett, is still due to his great name.

Instead of riots and destruction of property, Hampden clubs were now established in many of our large towns, and the villages and districts around them; Cobbett's books were printed in a cheap form; the labourers read them, and thenceforward became deliberate and systematic in their proceedings. Nor were there wanting men of their own class, to encourage and direct the new converts; the Sunday Schools of the preceding thirty years, had produced many working men of sufficient talent to become readers, writers, and speakers in the village meetings for parliamentary reform; some also were found to possess a rude poetic talent, which rendered their effusions popular, and bestowed an additional charm on their assemblages: and by such various means, anxious listeners at first, and then zealous proselytes, were drawn from the cottages of quiet nooks and dingles, to the weekly readings and discussions of the Hampden clubs. Samuel Bamford. *Passages in the Life of a Radical*, 1844, I, 6–8

The division of labour which both necessitated and was made necessary by factory development naturally increased the variety of specialised jobs. The stages of spinning production and some criteria for factory siting are here described by Ure.

41 The modern art of spinning cotton by machinery, which has long since supplanted that by the hand-wheel throughout civilized Europe and America, consists of the following operations:

1. The *cleaning* and opening up or loosening the flocks of cotton wool, as imported in the bags, so as to separate at once the coarser and heavier impurities as well as those of a lighter and finer kind.

2. The *carding*, which is intended to disentangle every tuft or knot, to remove every remaining impurity which might have eluded the previous operation, and finally to prepare for arranging the fibres in parallel lines, by laying the cotton first in a fleecy web, and then in a riband form.

3. The *doubling* and *drawing out* of the card-ends or ribands, in order to complete the parallelism of the filaments, and to equalize their quality and texture.

4. The *roving* operation, whereby the *drawings* made in the preceding process are greatly attenuated, with no more twist than is indispensable to preserve the uniform continuity of the spongy cards; which twist either remains in them, or is taken out immediately after the attenuation.

5. The *fine roving* and *stretching* come next; the former opera-

tion being effected by the fine bobbin-and-fly frame, the latter by the stretcher mule.

6. The *spinning* operation finishes the extension and twist of the yarn, and is done either in a continuous manner by the water twist and throstle, or discontinuously by the mule; in the former the yarn is progressively drawn, twisted, and wound up on the bobbins; in the latter it is drawn out and twisted in lengths of about 56 inches, which are then wound all at once upon the spindles.

7. The seventh operation is the *winding*, doubling, and singeing of the yarns, to fit them for the muslin, the stocking, or the bobbin-net lace manufacture.

8. The *packing-press*, for making up the yarn into bundles for the market, concludes this series.

9. To the above may be added the operations of the dressing-machines, and,

10. The power-looms.

The site of the factory ought to be carefully selected in reference to the health of the operatives, the cheapness of provisions, the facilities of transport for the raw materials, and the convenience of a market for the manufactured articles. An abundant supply of labour, as well as fuel and water for mechanical power, ought to be primary considerations in setting down a factory. It should therefore be placed, if possible, in a populous village, near a river or a canal, but in a situation free from marsh malaria, and with such a slope to the voider stream as may ensure the ready discharge of all liquid impurities. These circumstances happily conspire in the districts of Stockport, Hyde, Stayley Bridge, Duckenfield, Bury, Blackburn, &c., and have eminently favoured the rapid extension of the cotton manufactures for which these places are pre-eminent. Andrew Ure. *The Cotton Manufacture of Great Britain*, 1836, I, 294–5

Atmospheric conditions, local traditions, and the availability of labour, capital, and power, determined the concentration of the cotton industry. Here Baines lists the cotton areas of the mid-1830s. By this time the cotton industry throughout the Kingdom was using 110,000 power-looms—and by 1850 the total was 250,000.

---

42 The topography of the cotton manufacture and of its principal branches requires some observations. Five great districts may be specified as seats of the cotton manufacture:—1st. Manchester, with from thirty to fifty miles in every direction round it. 2d. Glasgow, the same, but extending to Perth, Aberdeen, and through many parts of the Highlands. 3d. Nottingham, taking in Derby, Warwick, Lichfield, &c. 4th. Carlisle, branching out in every direction, so as to meet the Manchester and Glasgow divisions. 5th. The Irish counties of Antrim, Armagh, Dublin, Kildare, and others to a small extent.

Of these, the Lancashire district is much more important, for the quantity, variety, and excellence of its productions, than all the others together. In that county, the original seat of the British cotton manufacture, the departments of spinning, manufacturing, bleaching, and printing, are all carried to the highest perfection. The Manchester mills supply the finest yarns for the manufacture of muslins at Glasgow, and of lace at Nottingham; and almost every description of cotton goods, except lace and hosiery, is made in Lancashire. Edward Baines. *History of the Cotton Manufacture in Great Britain*, 1835, 417

The Woollen and Worsted Industries During the early development of the factory system, the old woollen districts retained their traditional individual characteristics. As the Committee on the State of the Woollen Manufacture (see p 80) reported in 1806, there were varied stages of organisation. In the following passages the Committee describes the current state of the woollen industry in the major areas. Both domestic and factory systems received praise. 'Your Committee cannot participate in the apprehensions which are entertained by the domestic clothiers . . . the lively fears, of the decline of the domestic, and the general establishment of the factory system, may reasonably excite surprise . . . the quantity of cloth manufactured by the domestic system has increased immensely of late years, not only in itself but as compared with the quantity made in factories.' On such grounds the committee played down the alarm felt by some Yorkshire domestic workers at the growth of the factories.

---

43 . . . there are three different modes of carrying on the Woollen Manufacture; that of the Master Clothier of the West of England, the Factory, and, the Domestic System.

In all the Western Counties as well as in the North, there are Factories, but the Master Clothier of the West of England buys his Wool from the Importer, if it be Foreign, or in the Fleece, or of the Wool-stapler, if it be of Domestic growth; after which, in all the different processes through which it passes, he is under the necessity of employing as many distinct classes of persons; sometimes working in their own houses, sometimes in those of the Master Clothier, but none of them going out of their proper line. Each class of Workmen, however, acquires great skill in performing its particular operation, and hence may have arisen the acknowledged excellence, and, till of late, superiority, of the Cloths of the West of England. It is however a remarkable fact, of which Your Committee has been assured by one of its own Members, that previously to the introduction of Machinery, it was very common, and it is said sometimes to happen at this day, for the North Countryman to come into the West of England, and, in the Clothing Districts of that part of the Kingdom, to purchase his Wool, which he carries home; where, having worked it up into Cloth, he brings it back again, and sells it in its native District. This is supposed to arise from the Northern Clothier being at liberty to work himself, and employ his own family and others, in any way which his interest or convenience may suggest.

In the Factory system, the Master Manufacturers, who sometimes possess a very great capital, employ in one or more

Buildings or Factories, under their own or their Superintendant's inspection, a number of Workmen, more or fewer according to the extent of their Trade. This system, it is obvious, admits in practice of local variations. But both in the system of the West of England Clothier, and in the Factory system, the work, generally speaking, is done by persons who have no property in the goods they manufacture, for in this consists the essential distinction between the two former systems, and the Domestic.

In the last-mentioned, or Domestic system, which is that of Yorkshire, the Manufacture is conducted by a multitude of Master Manufacturers, generally possessing a very small, and scarcely ever any great extent of Capital. They buy the Wool of the Dealer; and, in their own houses, assisted by their wives and children, and from two or three to six or seven Journeymen, they dye it (when dyeing is necessary) and through all the different stages work it up into undressed Cloth.

Various processes however, the chief of which were formerly done by hand, under the Manufacturer's own roof, are now performed by Machinery, in public Mills, as they are called, which work for hire. There are several such Mills near every manufacturing Village, so that the Manufacturer, with little inconvenience or loss of time, carries thither his goods, and fetches them back again, when the process is completed. When it has attained to the state of undressed Cloth, he carries it on the Market-day to a public Hall or Market, where the Merchants repair to purchase.

Several thousands of these small Master Manufacturers attend the Market of Leeds, where there are three Halls for the exposure and sale of their Cloths: and there are other similar Halls, where the same system of selling in public Market prevails, at Bradford, Halifax, and Huddersfield. The Halls consist of long walks or galleries, throughout the whole length of which the Master Manufacturers stand in a double row, each behind his own little division or stand, as it is termed, on which his goods are exposed to sale. In the interval between these

rows the Merchants pass along, and make their purchases. At
the end of an hour, on the ringing of a bell, the Market closes,
and such Cloths as have been purchased are carried home to
the Merchants' houses; such Goods as remain unsold continuing
in the Halls till they find a purchaser at some ensuing Market.
It should however be remarked, that a practice has also obtained of late years, of Merchants giving out Samples to some
Manufacturer whom they approve, which Goods are brought
to the Merchant directly, without ever coming into the Halls.
These, however, no less than the others, are manufactured by
him in his own family. The greater Merchants have their
working-room, or, as it is termed, their Shop, in which their
Workmen, or, as they are termed, Croppers, all work together.
The Goods which, as it has been already stated, are bought in
the undressed state, here undergo various processes, till, being
completely finished, they are sent away for the use of the con-
sumer, either in the Home or the Foreign Market; the Merchants sending them abroad directly without the intervention
of any other Factor. Sometimes again the Goods are dressed at
a stated rate by Dressers, who take them in for that purpose.

The greater part of the Domestic Clothiers live in Villages
and detached houses, covering the whole face of a district of
from 20 to 30 miles in length, and from 12 to 15 in breadth.
Coal abounds throughout the whole of it; and a great proportion of the Manufacturers occupy a little Land, from 3 to 12 or
15 acres each. They often likewise keep a Horse, to carry their
Cloth to the Fulling Mill and the Market.

Though the system which has been just described be that
which has been generally established in the West Riding of
Yorkshire, yet there have long been a few Factories in the
neighbourhood of Halifax and Huddersfield; and four or five
more, one however of which has been since discontinued, have
been set on foot not many years ago in the neighbourhood of
Leeds. These have for some time been objects of great jealousy
to the Domestic Clothiers. The most serious apprehensions
have been stated, by Witnesses who have given their evidence

before Your Committee in behalf of the Domestic Manufacturers, lest the Factory system should gradually root out the Domestic; and lest the independent little Master Manufacturer, who works on his own account, should sink into a journeyman working for hire. It is for the purpose of counteracting this supposed tendency of the Factory system to increase, that a numerous class of Petitioners wish, instead of repealing, to amend and enforce the Act of Philip and Mary, for restricting the number of Looms to be worked in any one tenement; and with a similar view they wish to retain in force the 5th of Elizabeth, which enacts the system of Apprenticeships. . . .

Your Committee cannot wonder that the Domestic Clothiers of Yorkshire are warmly attached to their accustomed mode of carrying on the manufacture: It is not merely that they are *accustomed* to it—it obviously possesses many eminent advantages seldom found in a great manufacture.

It is one peculiar recommendation of the Domestic system of Manufacture, that, as it has been expressly stated to Your Committee, a young man of good character can always obtain credit for as much wool as will enable him to set up as a little Master Manufacturer, and the public Mills, which are now established in all parts of the Clothing District, and which work for hire, at any easy rate, enable him to command the use of very expensive and complicated Machines, the construction and necessary repairs of which would require a considerable capital. Thus, instances not unfrequently occur, wherein men rise from low beginnings, if not to excessive wealth, yet to a situation of comfort and independence.

It is another advantage of the Domestic system of Manufacture, and an advantage which is obviously not confined to the individuals who are engaged in it, but which, as well as other parts of this system, extends its benefits to the Landholder, that any sudden stoppage of a Foreign Market, any failure of a great House, or any other of those adverse shocks to which our Foreign Trade especially is liable, in its present extended state, has not the effect of throwing a great number of Workmen out of employ, as it often does, when the stroke falls on the Capital of a single individual. In the Domestic system, the loss is spread over a large superficies; it affects the whole body of the Manufacturers; and, though each little Master be a sufferer, yet few, if any, feel the blow so severely as to be altogether ruined. Moreover, it appears in evidence, that in such cases as these, they seldom turn off any of their standing set of Journeymen, but keep them at work in hopes of better times.

On the whole, Your Committee feel no little satisfaction in bearing their testimony to the merits of the Domestic system of Manufacture; to the facilities it affords to men of steadiness and industry to establish themselves as little Master Manufacturers, and to maintain their families in comfort by their own industry and frugality; and to the encouragement which it thus holds out to domestic habits and virtues. Neither can they omit to notice its favourable tendencies on the health and morals of a large and important class of the community.

But while your Committee thus freely recognize the merits and value of the Domestic system, they at the same time feel it their duty to declare it as their decided opinion, that the apprehensions entertained of its being rooted out by the Factory system, are, at present at least, wholly without foundation.

. . . On the whole, Your Committee do not wonder that the Domestic Clothiers are warmly attached to their peculiar system. This is a predilection in which the Committee participate; but at the same time they must declare, that they see at present no solid ground for the alarm which has gone forth, lest the Halls should be deserted, and the generality of Merchants should set up Factories. Your Committee, however, must not withhold the declaration, that if any such disposition had been perceived, it must have been their less pleasing duty to state, that it would by no means have followed, that it was a disposition to be counteracted by positive law.   Report from the Committee on the State of the Woollen Manufacture of England, *Parliamentary Papers*, 1806, III, 8–9, 10, 12   _____

Among many tourists who published descriptions of their travels through the industrial areas was Sir George Head (1782–1855). He recorded his impressions of the Yorkshire woollen towns in 1835 in some detail. While noting the dirt of the factory areas, he was in general favourably impressed. The woollen and worsted industries were now starting a period of rapid mechanisation: the number of power looms rose from 5,000 to 42,000 between 1835 and 1850 and the number of factory employees from 55,000 to 154,000. Head was a soldier in the commissariat and was knighted for his work at the coronation of King William IV. He supplemented his *Home Tour* with a *Home Tour through various parts of the United Kingdom in 1837*, republishing both works together in 1840.

---

44 The manufactures of Halifax are various—comprising articles of cotton and woollen cloths, but chiefly merinos and the finer sorts of worsted. . . .

The town of Dewsbury is not only celebrated for its manufacture of blankets, but also for a novel business or trade which has sprung up in England, in addition to the arts and sciences, of late years—namely, that of grinding old garments new;— literally tearing in pieces fusty old rags, collected from Scotland, Ireland, and the Continent, by a machine called the 'devil', till a substance very like the original wool is reproduced; this, by the help of a small addition of new wool, is respun and manufactured into sundry useful coarse articles. . . . A single glance at the ceremony going forward [in a shoddy mill at Batley Carr] was quite sufficient to convey a tolerable idea of the business,—a single whiff of air from the interior of the apartment was almost more than could be endured. . . .

There is no manufacturing town in England, I should imagine, wherein more coal is consumed, in proportion to its extent, than Leeds. . . . The sun himself is obscured by smoke, as by a natural mist. . . .

. . . Instead of regarding [the manufacturer] as an individual on whom hundreds, nay thousands of his fellow-creatures depend for their daily bread, expressions of morbid sympathy have, on the contrary, never ceased to paint the situation of the operatives far darker than it is in reality. . . .

With respect to the general state of the workmen, and especially the children in the factories, I certainly gained, by personal inspection, a happy release from opinions previously entertained; neither could I acknowledge those resemblances, probably the work of interested artists, by whom such touching portraits of misery and overfatigue had been from time to time embellished; I saw around me wherever I moved, on every side, a crowd of apparently happy beings, working in lofty well-ventilated buildings, with whom a comparison could no more in fairness be drawn with the solitary weaver plying his shuttle from morning to night in his close dusty den, than is the bustle and occupation of life with soul-destroying solitude.   Sir George Head. *A Home Tour through the Manufacturing Districts of England, in the Summer of 1835*, 1836, 123–4, 144, 146, 169, 186–7

In the winter of 1849–1850 the 'Peelite' *Morning Chronicle* published a series of reports by 'special correspondents' on Labour and the Poor in the Metropolitan, Rural, and Manufacturing Districts of England and Wales. The London series was written by the celebrated Henry Mayhew, and the agricultural and industrial authors have been recognised as Alexander Mackay and Angus Reach respectively. In the following extracts Reach describes various sections of the West Riding woollen industry in the mid-nineteenth century. Despite the growth of the factory system, much work was still performed by home-workers, as Reach observes.

45   THE CLOTH DISTRICTS OF YORKSHIRE
LETTER XIV

The town of Huddersfield is a species of minor capital of the broad and fancy cloth-working districts of Yorkshire; Leeds being taken as the general manufacturing metropolis of the county. In Huddersfield and its neighbourhood, however, a very important proportion of the cloth-working of the entire district is carried on, and much of the fine-textured stuffs, conventionally known as "West of England goods", is spun, woven, and finished on the banks of the Colne. The town of Huddersfield contains rather more than 36,000, and the district comprehended by the Huddersfield union is peopled by somewhat more than 108,000 inhabitants. The number of paupers at present accommodated in the several workhouses of the union amounts to about 250, and the amount of out-door relief granted during a single week in the beginning of the present month was £186. In the year 1846, out of 939 couples who married, 378 men and 696 women signed the register with their marks. The value of life in Huddersfield, as stated in the Registrar's General Report, is 1 in 49 as regards males, and 1 in 52 as regards females; showing a degree of mortality less by nearly 10 per cent than that of Chorley, the healthiest of the cotton towsn.

The population of Huddersfield and the surrounding districts are almost entirely engaged in the manufacture of wool—the scattered cotton and silk spinning and weaving establishments which may be found here and there being merely exceptions to the general rule. By far the greater part of the woollen manufacture of Huddersfield is carried on, in all its stages, in the mills. When weaving is put out, the work is generally executed by country people living within a circuit of some half-dozen miles. The species of fabric so manufactured is commonly that distinguished, in its different kinds, as fancy goods. The Ten Hours Bill applies to woollen factories just as it does to cotton mills. In the woollen districts, however, there seems to have been no attempt made to get rid of its restrictions. No mill, so far as my inquiries have extended, has sought to work by means of the relay system; and in the vast majority of instances, at least so far as regards the woollen in opposition to the worsted trade, no children are employed until they are above thirteen years of age.

The town of Huddersfield belongs to one ground landlord—Sir John Ramsden. No building leases are granted, and the in-

L

habitants are therefore, *pro tanto*, tenants at will The town has sprung up almost entirely within the last sixty years. Previous to that time it was but an insignificant cluster of irregularly built lanes. The small manufacturers around brought in their wares upon packhorses, and on the market-day exposed them for sale on the churchyard-wall. When the Cloth Hall was opened, many of these humble producers had not sufficient capital to rent a stall. Although thus comparatively a new town, Huddersfield is by no means a well-built town. . . .

I have already sketched the principal features of the long-staple woollen manufacture—my information being derived from a careful inspection of several of the mills, great and small, in Huddersfield and in the surrounding district. The processes of converting the wool into broadcloth or fancy goods are carried on both in and out of the mills; but the strong tendency of the trade is to concentrate itself in the factories under the eyes of the proprietors, who very generally complain of the dilatoriness of the home workmen, and the uncertainty of their completing their tasks by the stipulated time. The workpeople, on the other hand, maintain that they suffer from the caprice of the employers in bestowing work, and from the frequency with which they are compelled to make repeated journeys to the warehouses or mills before they obtain the yarn which they are to spin and weave in their own homes.

The houses inhabited by the factory hands of Huddersfield consist in most cases of a large parlour-kitchen opening from the street, with a cellar beneath it, and either two small bedrooms or one large one above. In some instances a scullery is added to the main apartment. The general style of furniture is much the same as that which distinguished the operative dwellings of the cotton districts. If there be any difference, I should say that that of Huddersfield seems the more plainly substantial of the two. The clock and the corner cupboards, and the shelves glittering with ranges of dishes and plates, are to be found as universally as in Manchester, and a plentiful supply of good water is in general conducted into every house.

Taking wages as the test of social condition, the operatives of Huddersfield may be considered as very fairly situated. Children below 13 years of age are seldom employed in the mills, and the average earnings of those over that age may be 5s. weekly. The earnings of the women may vary from 7s. or thereabouts— obtained by those who pick and boil—to 9s. or 10s., or thereabouts, obtained by those who weave. The average may be about 8s. 6d. The average wage of the women is raised by the number of their sex who work at the loom, as the average wage of the men is depressed by the same cause. Slubbers, carders, spinners, dyers, fullers, raisers, and finishers may average about 18s. a week. Taking into account the number of adult males employed as weavers, both by power and hand, the general average sinks, and may be placed at from 14s. to 15s. per week. Admitting these estimates to be generally correct, the average wage earned by adults in Huddersfield may be placed at 11s. 6d. a week—an amount very similar to the general run of wages in the cotton districts, while the average earned by all sexes and ages may be estimated at something more than 9s. . . . The rents paid range from £7 to £8, or about 3s. per week.

The yarns given out by the mills to be spun and woven at the homes of the workpeople, are taken to the rural districts around, or to the remote suburbs of Huddersfield. At a little village called Paddock, about a mile from the town, a number of looms are generally going. Proceeding there, I entered upon a series of domiciliary visits. The general arrangements of the houses were similar. The looms invariably occupied the first floor. In some cases, one and two uncurtained beds, almost invariably left unmade, were placed in corners. In other instances, the sleeping arrangements were upon the ground-floor, or within a third chamber roughly partitioned off from the loom apartment. . . .

In another house I found that only two people resided, a man and his wife. . . . There were two looms here for the husband and wife. The man, who was busy, stopped his shuttle to speak to me. For the cloth which he was weaving he could have got, seven years ago, 10d. a yard; the price now paid was only 4½d. When he had pretty regular work, his average weekly earnings were about 10s. For this he frequently worked from six o'clock in the morning until eight o'clock at night. Last summer trade had been bad with him, and one week with another he had not much above 8s. The earnings of his wife generally amounted to about 3s. 6d. per week. Taking an average, he thought that their united earnings might be about 12s. 6d. or 13s. a week. This was when trade was tolerably good. Sometimes they could not make more than 10s. a week between them. He paid for his house £8 10s. per annum. The poor-rates were 6s. 3d.; the highway rates, 3s. 3½d.; and the charge for water 5s. The woollen hand-loom weavers about Huddersfield were very ill-off. "If they have young families", said the woman, "that is, families over young to help them by working in the mills, they don't get half enough to eat." . . .

The small town of Dewsbury holds, in the woollen district, very much the same position which Oldham does in the cotton country. The reader will remember that an essential feature in the manufacture of the latter town is the spinning and preparing of waste and refuse cotton. To this stuff the name of shoddy is given; but the real and orthodox shoddy is a production of the woollen districts, and consists of the second-hand wool manufactured by the tearing up, or rather the grinding, of woollen rags by means of coarse willows, called devils; the operation of which sends forth choking clouds of dry pungent dirt and floating fibres. The real and original "devil's dust" having been, by the agency of the machinery in question, reduced to something like the original raw material, fresh wool is added to the pulp, in different proportions, according to the quality of the stuff to be manufactured, and the mingled material is at length reworked in the usual way into a coarse and little serviceable cloth.

There are some shoddy mills in the neighbourhood of Huddersfield; but the mean little town of Dewsbury may be taken as the metropolis of the manufacture, and thither I accordingly proceeded. The first mill I visited was that belonging to the Messrs. Blakely, in the immediate outskirts of the town. This establishment is devoted solely to the sorting, preparing, and grinding of rags, which are worked up in the neighbouring factories. Great bales choke-full of filthy tatters lay scattered about the yard, and loaded waggons were fast arriving, and adding to the heap. As for the mill, a glance at its exterior showed its character. It being a calm still day, the walls and part of the roof were covered with the thick clinging dust and fibre, which ascended in choky volumes from the open doors and glassless windows of the ground floor, and which also poured forth from a chimney, constructed for the purpose, exactly like smoke. On a windy day I was told that the appearance of the place would be by no means so bad, as a thorough draft would carry the dust rapidly away to leeward. As it was, however, the mill was covered as with a mildewy fungus, and upon the grey slates of the roof the frowzy deposit could not be less than two inches in depth.

We went first into the upper story, where the rags are stored. A great wareroom was piled in many places from the floor to the ceiling with bales of woollen rags, torn strips and tatters of every colour peeping out from the bursting depositaries. There is hardly a country in Europe which does not contribute its quota of material to the shoddy manufacturer. Rags are brought from France, Germany, and in great quantities from Belgium. Denmark, I understand, is favourably looked upon by the tatter-merchants, being fertile in morsels of clothing, of fair quality. Of domestic rags, the Scotch bear off the palm; and possibly no one will be surprised to hear, that of all rags Irish rags are the most worn, the filthiest, and generally the most unprofitable. . . .

Under the rag wareroom was the sorting and picking room. Here the bales are opened, and their contents piled in close poverty-smelling masses, upon the floor. The operatives were entirely women. They sat upon low stools, or half sunk and half enthroned amid heaps of the filthy goods, busily employed in arranging them according to the colour and the quality of the morsels, and from the more pretending quality of rags carefully ripping out every particle of cotton which they could detect. Piles of rags of different sorts, dozens of feet high, were the obvious fruits of their labour. All these women were over eighteen years of age, and the wages which they were paid for ten hours' work were 6s. per week. They looked squalid and dirty enough, but all of them were chattering, and several singing, over their noisome labour. The atmosphere of the room was close and oppressive; and although I perceived no particularly offensive smell, we could not help being sensible of the presence of a choky, mildewy sort of odour—a hot, moist exhalation—arising from the sodden smouldering piles, as the workwomen tossed armfuls of rags from one heap to another. In this mill, and at this species of work—the lowest and foulest which any phase of the factory system can show—I found, for the first time, labouring as regular mill-hands, Irish women.

The devils were, as I have said, upon the ground-floor. The choking dust burst out from door and window, and it was not until a minute or so that I could see the workmen, moving amid clouds, catching up armfuls of the sorted rags, and tossing them into the machine to be torn into fibry fragments by the whirling revolutions of its spiky teeth. So far as I could make out, the place was a large bare room—the uncovered beams above, the rough stone walls, and the woodwork of the unglazed windows being, as it were, furred over with clinging woolly matter. On the floor, the dust and coarse filaments lay as if—to use the quaint phrase of a gentleman present—"it had been snowing snuff". The workmen were of course coated with the flying powder. They wore bandages over their mouths, so as to prevent as much as possible the inhalation of the dust, and seemed loth to remove the protection for a moment. Not one of them, however, would admit that he found the trade injurious. . . .

In Batley I went over two shoddy establishments—the Bridge Mill and the Albion Mill. In both of these rags were not only ground, but the shoddy was worked up into coarse bad cloth, a great proportion of which is sent to America for slave clothing. In one of the mills in question, the two rag-grinders at work were Irishwomen whom I have mentioned. They laboured in a sort of half-roofed outhouse, the floor littered with rags and heaped with dust, the walls and beams furred with wavy down-like masses of filament, as though they had been imbedded in clusters of cobweb; while the air, stirred by the revolving cylinders and straps, was a perfect whirlwind of pungent titilating powder. Through this the women, with their squalid dust-strewn garments, powdered to a dull greyish hue, and with their bandages tied over the greater part of their faces, moved like reanimated mummies in their swathings: I had seldom seen anything more ghastly. The wages of these poor creatures do not exceed 7s. or 8s. a week. The men are much better paid, none of them making less than 18s. a week, and many earning as much as 22s. . . .

. . . The weaving is, for the most part, carried on at the homes of the workpeople. I visited several at Batley Car. The domestic arrangements consisted, in every case, of two tolerably large rooms, one above the other, with a cellar beneath—a plan of construction called in Yorkshire a "house and a chamber". The chamber had generally a bed amid the looms. The weavers were, as usual, complaining of irregular work and diminished wages. Their average pay, one week with another, with their wives to wind for them—*i.e.*, to place the thread upon the bobbin which goes into the shuttle—is hardly so much as 10s. a week. They work long hours, often fourteen per day. In one or two instances I found the weaver a small capitalist, with perhaps half a dozen looms, and a hand-jenny for spinning thread, the workpeople being within his own family as regular apprentices and journeymen.

. . . "Shoddy fever", is, in fact, a modification of the very fatal disease induced by what is called "dry grinding" at Sheffield; but of course the particles of woollen filaments are less fatal in their influence than the floating steel-dust produced by the operation in question. The value of life in the Dewsbury dis-

trict is about 1 in 47. It is always to be distinctly understood
that the rag-grinders constitute an exceedingly trifling minority
of the workpeople employed. The operations which succeed
that in which the devil plays the most prominent part, seem to
be just as healthy as in those mills which prepare from the finer
wools the finer cloths.

[Monday, Dec. 3, 1849.]
Supplement to the Morning Chronicle, 18 Jan 1850

LETTER XV

. . . When "stuffs" are woven, they may—except, perhaps, for
the operations of the dye-house—be considered as ready for
sale, such fabrics not involving the multiform finishing processes necessary in the production of glossy broadcloth.

So much for the technical differences between woollen cloths
and stuffs. In these differences are involved matters tending to
produce, to a very considerable extent, different social phases
amid the workpeople. Stuff manufacture is a much cleaner
trade than woollen manufacture. Stuff mills rival, if they do not
surpass, silk mills in cleanliness and coolness, and sweetness of
atmosphere. The dye is rarely applied until the fabric is turned
out of the factory. There is little or no oil used in, or evolved by,
the process. No high temperature is requisite, at least so far as
the mills go; and altogether the work carried on in the stuff
factories is well calculated to exhibit in the most favourable
light the physical condition of the labourers. Notwithstanding
all this, however, the stuff manufacturers are worse off than the
woollen manufacturers, when tried by the grand test of the
labourer's condition—his wages. In the stuff-mills there are
employed, at the very least, a score of women, boys, and
children, to one man. The adult males employed at the
machinery are either the few who are overlookers, or the rather
larger number who are forced to compete with women and
girls at the power-loom. The great bulk of the male worsted
population work at the unwholesome, easily acquired, and
miserably paid for—because easily learned—labour of wool-

combing. Thus the average of wages is kept lower than in the cotton and cloth, and about as low perhaps as in the silk, districts. The average wages of adult male workmen engaged in the stuff trade cannot be above 10s. a week, at the most liberal estimate. That of women ranges closely up to them; for a female weaver will earn as much, or more, than a male comber. And as for the children, the average of the wages which they receive is kept down by the great number of "half-timers"—boys and girls under thirteen years of age—who are employed. Exclusive of half-time workers and young persons, the average weekly wages of male and female adults may be reckoned at from 8s. 6d. to 9s. 6d.—lower by about 2s. 6d. than the average wages in the cotton districts, reckoning in both cases on a time of fair prosperity, and a period of ten hours' daily toil.

Halifax and Bradford are . . . the centres of the stuff manufacture. The former town possesses, however, other industrial resources than that of the staple trade. The mayor, Mr. Crossley, for instance, is the chief partner in an immense carpet manufacturing establishment, employing about 1,500 hands, principally adult males, and paying about £1,000 weekly in wages. Besides this and other establishments of different kinds, the worsted manufacturers of Halifax prepare so great a variety of the staple production, that periods of distress fall in general lighter upon them than on their Bradford neighbours. The latter town is, perhaps, more quickly and keenly affected by the variations of trade than any other manufacturing depot in England. The masters are generally reputed as bold speculators; and the mill owner who ventures his money freely, hazards, of necessity, the wages of his people as well as his own profits. In Halifax, however, things are conducted more slowly and quietly. Compared with Bradford, the place has a touch of antiquity in its aspect and its tone. So far as appearance goes, no two towns can be more dissimilar. Halifax is an ancient borough, girdled by an *enceint* of mills and mill-hands' dwellings. Bradford seems spick and span new from the centre to the circumference. There are points in the town of Halifax, from

which the gazer will be put in mind of the quaint cities of
Normandy and Bavaria—Rouen or Bamberg—so steep and
narrow are the streets, and so picturesque the plaster walls,
streaked with chequering beams of blackened wood—the
numerous street-turned gables—the ledge-like stories, each
overhanging the other—and the grey and time-tarnished hue
of the great coarse slates which form the high crow-footed and
ridgy roofs. . . .

Mr. Smith, of Deanston, in a sanitary report made about
1837, describes Bradford as being the dirtiest town in England.
Mr. Smith must have written ere he extended his researches to
Halifax. At all events, Bradford is rapidly improving. . . .

The first factory in Halifax which I visited was that of the
Messrs. Holdsworth. It is a vast establishment, weaving all
manner of stuff goods, situated upon the outskirts of the town,
and surrounded by the dwellings of the workpeople. The active
and energetic chief of the firm conducted me through the
works. The weaving shed is one of the noblest structures of the
kind I have ever seen, perfectly lighted, not only by ordinary
windows, but by means of a species of serrated roof, the perpen-
dicular portions of which are glass. That the arrangements for
ventilation are excellent, was sufficiently proved by the perfectly fresh state of the atmosphere, and the workpeople
laboured with spirit and energy. There were a few Jacquard
looms in the shed, but the greater number were of the ordinary
kind. There might have been about one man to every ten
women and girls. The wages of the former average 10s., those
of the latter 8s. weekly.

In estimating the remuneration of workpeople, I am frequently puzzled to reconcile the statements of the operatives
and those of their masters, and yet I believe both to be grounded
on fact. Where the amount of wages fluctuates with the skill of
the workman and the quality of the fabric wrought, two parties
looking at the question from different points of view will almost
invariably state results each of which is capable of being supported by figures representing the sums earned or the sums

paid, but neither giving a really fair view of the case. The master will frequently strike an average from what his best hands working at the best jobs may earn. The labourer will just as frequently base his calculations upon what the most ordinary hands working on the most ordinary jobs do receive. In neither case can you complain of absolute want of truth, but in both cases you will have to lament an equal absence of candour. . . .

To return to the workpeople of Messrs. Holdsworth's factory. The vast majority of weavers were young women. In neatness and propriety of dress they rivalled the silk spinners, and shawls and bonnets were hung along the walls, as I have described them in Macclesfield. In a smaller spinning room the machinery ran quicker—so quickly, indeed, as to cause a perceptible tremor in the building; and here the wages of the workwomen ranged somewhat higher. To be removed to the quick spinning room was to be promoted. In the carding, drawing, and spinning departments, the mechanism was almost exclusively looked after by young women and girls, at the low wages of 5s. and 5s. 5d. The men employed were overlookers, and earned from 15s. to 22s. The ventilation in these rooms was hardly so good as in the weaving shed, but still I cannot say that there was much to complain of. The girls looked hale and hearty, and Mr. Holdsworth was energetic in calling my attention to their plumpness, a quality which, in a large majority of cases, they certainly possessed to a very fair degree. . . .

. . . From the Messrs. Holdsworth's mill I proceeded to another—that of the Messrs. Ackroyd. The average wages paid in this establishment were thus stated to me by a very intelligent overlooker. The adult males, not including the weavers, might have about 17s. a week; female adults might average, in the spinning and drawing rooms, about 6s. or 6s. 3d.; young persons from 13 to 18, about 4s. 9d.; and children from 8 to 13, working five hours a day, from 1s. 9d. to 2s. 3d. In the weaving department my informant thought that the average rate earned by men and women might be somewhat above 8s. per week. As in the case of the former mill, the factory in question was kept as clean as possible. . . .

. . . Of course there are a great number of woolcombers in Halifax, but the account which I shall give of these workmen in Bradford will suffice for both.

Let us now proceed, then, to the latter place. In an architectural point of view, the best features of Bradford consist of numerous ranges of handsome warehouses. The streets have none of the old-fashioned picturesqueness of those of Halifax. The best of them are muddy, and not too often swept. Mills abound in great plenty, and their number is daily increasing, while the town itself extends in like proportion. Bradford is, as I have said, essentially a new town. Half a century ago it was a mere cluster of huts: now the district of which it is the heart contains upwards of 132,000 inhabitants. The value of life is about 1 in 40. Fortunes have been made in Bradford with a rapidity almost unequalled even in the manufacturing districts. In half a dozen years men have risen from the loom to possess mills and villas. At present, stuff manufacturers are daily pouring into the town from Leeds; while a vast proportion of the wool-combing of the empire seems, as it were, to have concentrated itself in Bradford. . . .

As I have hinted, the Bradford employers are, in the slang of the manufacturing districts, accounted "high-pressure men". I have been told that a mere spirit of rapid demand is sufficient to cause loom-shed after loom-shed to arise. The fabrics manufactured being also of the same general class, their sale increases and diminishes simultaneously; and the consequence is, that every shade of variation in the market means hundreds of dinners the more or the less in Bradford. A town of this class is just one of those on which, in prosperous seasons, the flood of agricultural pauperism bears down. Trade is at present exceedingly brisk in Bradford—so brisk that even stables are put into requisition to contain the wool, for lack of warehouse room. . . .

. . . As I have stated, the greatest part of the labour of male adults through the worsted districts consists in combing wool. In Bradford I was told, on good authority, that there are about 15,000 woolcombers. These men sometimes work singly, but more often three, four, or five, club together and labour in what is called a shop, generally consisting of the upper room or "chamber" over the lower room or "house". Their wives and children assist them to a certain extent in the first and almost unskilled portions of the operation, but the whole process is rude and easily acquired. It consists of forcibly pulling the wool through metal combs or spikes, of different lengths, and set five or six deep. These combs must be kept at a high temperature, and consequently the central apparatus in a combing room is always a "fire-pot", burning either coke, coals, or charcoal, and constructed so as to allow three, four, or five combs to be heated at it; the vessel being in these cases respectively called a "pot o' three", a "pot o' four", or a "pot o' five". When coals are burned, the pot is a fixed apparatus, like a small stove, with a regular funnel to carry away the smoke. When charcoal is used, the pot is a movable vessel, without a funnel, the noxious fumes too often spreading freely in the room. Scattered through the chamber are frequently two or more poles or masts, to which the combs, after being heated, are firmly attached, while the workman drags the wool through them until he has reduced it to a soft mass of filament—when he educes the substance as it were, draws it by skilful manipulation out of the compact lump into long semi-transparent "slivers", which, after certain minor operations, are returned to the factory to be subjected to the "drawing machines". The general aspect of a combing-room may therefore be described as that of a bare chamber, heated to nearly 85 degrees. A round fire-pot stands in the centre; masses of wool are heaped about; and four or five men, in their shirt-sleeves, are working busily.

... Woolcombers' hours are, I believe, proverbially long. The men in Bradford said they were sometimes forced to work most of the night. Low as their wages are, they were recently still lower; but since the revival of trade in the district, the wool-

combers have raised the amount of their remuneration upwards of 3s. by three successive strikes. The combers have now
to compete with machinery. Each machine will do about ten
times the work of a hand labourer, but it employs several
hands, two of whom get good wages. These machines are in
general, however, only used for the coarsest work, and did not
seem to excite any great apprehension among the workmen.
Woolcombing is the only branch of manufacturing industry
which I have yet met with supporting a fair proportion of adult
Irish males. A number of them have been bred to the employment at Mount Mellick, in Queen's County. The mass of the
woolcombers of Yorkshire includes natives of almost all the
southern counties of England. One and all, they were loud in
their denunciations of the accommodation provided for their
labour. In the south the masters used to provide shops for the
work. Here the men had to labour in their houses, and often to
sleep in the room in which they toiled. . . .

[Thursday, Dec. 6, 1849]
Supplement to the Morning Chronicle, 22 Jan 1850

Change in the West   The development of Yorkshire's woollen and worsted industries in the coal-rich West Riding inevitably harmed the East Anglian and Western textile districts.
William Cobbett (1763–1835), soldier, farmer, traditionalist,
Radical, journalist and MP for Oldham 1832–5, here describes
the declining state of some old woollen towns in 1826. Between
1821 and 1832 he visited twenty-seven counties in England,
publishing his impressions in his celebrated *Political Register*
periodical. In 1830 these reports, with their unique combina-
tion of Tory sentiment and Radical outrage, were largely republished in *Rural Rides*. The following extracts are taken from
the 1893 edition, edited by the Rev Pitt Cobbett.

---

46   [Salisbury, 30 August, 1826]
The villages down this Valley of Avon, and, indeed, it was

the same in almost every part of this county, and in the north and west of Hampshire also, used to have great employment for the women and children in the carding and spinning of wool for the making of broad-cloth. This was a very general employ-ment for the women and girls; but it is now wholly gone; and this has made a vast change in the condition of the people, and in the state of property and of manners and of morals. In 1816, I wrote and published a *Letter to the Luddites*, the object of which was to combat their hostility to the use of machinery. The arguments I there made use of were general. I took the matter in the abstract. The *principles* were all correct enough; but their application cannot be universal; and we have a case here before us, at this moment, which, in my opinion, shows that the mechanic inventions, pushed to the extent that they have been, have been productive of great calamity to this country, and that they will be productive of still greater calamity; unless, indeed, it be their brilliant destiny to be the immediate cause of putting an end to the present system.

The greater part of manufactures consists of *clothing* and *bed-ding*. Now, if by using a machine, we can get our coat with less labour than we got it before, the machine is a desirable thing. But, then, mind, we must have the machine at home, and we ourselves must have the profit of it; for if the machine be else-where; if it be worked by other hands; if other persons have the profit of it; and if, in consequence of the existence of the machine, we have hands at home who have nothing to do, and whom we must keep, then the machine is an injury to us, how-ever advantageous it may be to those who use it, and whatever traffic it may occasion with foreign states.

Such is the case with regard to this cloth-making. The machines are at Upton-Level, Warminster, Bradford, West-bury, and Trowbridge, and here are some of the hands in the Valley of Avon. This valley raises food and clothing; but in order to raise them it must have *labourers*. These are absolutely necessary; for without them this rich and beautiful valley becomes worth nothing except to wild animals and their pursuers. The labourers are *men* and *boys*. Women and girls occasionally; but the men and the boys are as necessary as the light of day, or as the air and the water. Now if beastly Malthus, or any of his nasty disciples, can discover a mode of having men and boys without having women and girls, then, certainly, the machine must be a good thing; but if this valley must absolutely have the women and the girls, then the machine, by leaving them with nothing to do, is a mischievous thing and a producer of most dreadful misery. . . .

[Warminster (Wilts.), 1 Sept. 1826]

I set out from Heytesbury this morning about six o'clock. Last night, before I went to bed, I found that there were some men and boys in the house who had come all the way from Bradford, about twelve miles, in order to get *nuts*. These people were men and boys that had been employed in the *cloth factories* at Bradford and about Bradford. I had some talk with some of these nutters, and I am quite convinced, not that the cloth making is at an *end*, but that it *never will be again what it has been*. Before last Christmas these manufacturers had full work, at one shilling and threepence a yard at broad-cloth weaving. They have now a quarter work, at one shilling a yard! One and threepence a yard for this weaving has been given at all times within the memory of man! Nothing can show more clearly than this, and in a stronger light, the great change which has taken place in the *remuneration for labour*. There was a turn out last winter, when the price was reduced to a shilling a yard; but it was put an end to in the usual way; the constable's staff, the bayonet, the gaol. . . .

[Sept. 2 1826]

[Frome] appears to be a sort of little Manchester. A very small Manchester, indeed; for it does not contain above ten to twelve thousand people, but it has all the *flash* of a Manchester, and the innkeepers and their people look and behave like the Manchester fellows. I was, I must confess, glad to find proofs of the irretrievable decay of the place. I remembered how ready the bluff manufacturers had been to *call in the troops* of various descriptions. "Let them", said I to myself, "call the troops in now, to make their trade revive. . . ."....

. . . The first factories that I met with were at a village called Upton Lovell, just before I came to Heytesbury. There they were a doing not more than a quarter work. There is only one factory, I believe, here at Warminster, and that has been suspended, during the harvest, at any rate. At Frome they are all upon about a quarter work. It is the same at Bradford and Trowbridge; and, as curious a thing as ever was heard of in the world is, that here are, through all these towns, and throughout this country, weavers from the north, singing about the towns ballads of Distress! . . .

[Ryall (Worcs.), 29 Sept. 1826]

I have observed, in this country, and especially near Worcester, that the working people seem to be better off than in many other parts, one cause of which is, I dare say, that *glove manufacturing*, which cannot be carried on by fire or by wind or by water, and which is, therefore, carried on by the *hands* of human beings. It gives work to women and children as well as to men; and that work is, by a great part of the women and children, done in their cottages, and amidst the fields and hop-gardens, where the husbands and sons must live, in order to raise the food and the drink and the wool. This is a great thing for the land. If this glove-making were to cease, many of these women and children, now not upon the parish, must instantly be upon the parish. The glove-trade is, like all others, slack from this last change in the value of money; but there is no horrible misery here, as at Manchester, Leeds, Glasgow, Paisley, and other Hell-Holes of 84 degrees of heat. There misery walks abroad in skin, bone and nakedness. There are no subscriptions wanted for Worcester; no militia-clothing. The working-people suffer, trades-people suffer, and who is to escape, except the monopolisers, the Jews, and the tax-eaters, when the government chooses to raise the value of money and lower the price of goods? The whole of the industrious part of the country must suffer in such a case; but where manufactur-

M

ing is mixed with agriculture, where the wife and daughters are at the needle, or the wheel, while the men and the boys are at the plough, and where the manufacturing, of which one or two towns are the centres, is spread over the whole country round about, and particularly where it is, in very great part, performed by females at their *own homes*, and where the earnings come *in aid of the man's wages*; in such case the misery cannot be so great; and accordingly, while there is an absolute destruction of life going on in the hell-holes, there is no *visible* misery at, or near, Worcester; and I cannot take my leave of this county without observing, that I do not recollect to have seen one miserable object in it. The working people all seem to have good large gardens, and pigs in their styes; and this last, say the *feelosofers* what they will about her "antallectual enjoyments", is the *only* security for happiness in a labourer's family.   William Cobbett. *Rural Rides*, 1893 edn, II, 78–80, 95, 103, 105, 163–4

Writing in 1842, at the depths of a cyclical depression, James Bischoff (1775–1845) described the Western woollen—and other—industries at a particularly bleak time. A Leeds and London merchant, he had for long been a prominent spokesman of the Yorkshire woollen interests, often seeing a cure for contemporary ills in the liberal panacea of free trade. The decline of the Western industry here described by no means obliterated the region's textile manufactures.

47 ... It is not civil and religious liberty alone that are essential to the prosperity of manufactures and trade; we have seen that they have been transferred from place to place in the same country, even in our own country, where those inestimable blessings extend to all classes, the highest and the lowest. Districts and towns have been enumerated where they once flourished and are now unknown, and these changes have taken place in the memory of men now living. Great changes are still in progress, and it is most distressing to see the accounts of the state of those counties so lately celebrated for the manu-

facture of the finest fabrics. Mr. Edwards, at a public meeting
at Bath in the month of January, 1842, stated—"At Bradford,
in Wilts, the decrease of the manufacture of broad cloth, which
is the staple commodity, is of a nature that is almost beyond
belief. About the year 1820 nineteen manufacturers carried on
business there, producing the aggregate of 620 pieces of broad
cloth per week; the town was at that period in a happy and
prosperous state as regarded the labouring population; every
family had employment, and their wages were good; fifteen
shillings per week was the usual price of a man's labour, whilst
weavers and other artisans earned still higher wages. The
contrast now is of such a nature as it is fearful to contemplate,
and such as I almost hesitate to declare. The manufacturers have
diminished to two in number, and the quantity reduced to one
hundred pieces, or one-sixth of the quantity made twenty years
ago. The change has not been the effect of any sudden convulsion,—it has been slow and gradual, one after another have
dropped away."

TABULAR VIEW OF THE MILL PROPERTY IN
THE COUNTY OF GLOUCESTER

District	Mills at Work		Not now used for Cloth	Void Mills	Rental		Loss of Rent
	1831	*1841*			*1831*	*1841*	
					£	£	£
Chalford ⎫ Painswick ⎬ Stroud ⎭	100	63	7	30	22,919	9,480	13,439
Uley	5	1	1	3	2,970	70	2,900
Wotton	20	11	2	7	3,600	1,045	2,555
Dursley	8	2	0	6	1,600	310	1,290
	133	77	10	46	31,089	10,905	20,184

It is needless, it is heart-rending, to pursue this most sad
description; sufficient has been said to confirm the statement,
that wherever advantage is offered, to those places the manu-

facture will go. The lamentable change, so far as respects the West of England, is caused by other districts possessing greater advantages; but the decline in the woollen manufacture has extended to more favoured countries, and it becomes an important question, whether the difference in the price of food be not the main, almost the whole, cause of the decline, not of the woollen manufactures alone, but of the cotton manufacture, and almost every other branch of the national industry in Great Britain.   James Bischoff. *A Comprehensive History of the Woollen and Worsted Manufactures and the Natural and Commercial History of Sheep, from the earliest records to the present period,* 1842, II, 434–6

_____

The New Factories   Factory design was regularly improved, as employers and architects learned how to overcome the cramped conditions and production bottlenecks of the early mills. In the following extract Ure describes Orrell's cotton factory at Stockport. He was obviously impressed by the building and wrote of it again in 1836.

_____

48   The building consists of a main body, and two lateral wings; the former being three hundred feet long, and fifty feet wide; the latter projecting fifty-eight feet in front of the body. There are seven stories, including the attics. The moving power consists of two eighty-horse steam-engines, working rectangularly together, which are mounted with their great gearing-wheels on the ground floor, at the end of the body opposite the spectator's right hand, and are separated by a strong wall from the rest of the building. . . .

The boilers for supplying steam to the engines, and to the warming-pipes of the building, are erected in an exterior building at the right-hand end of the mill; and transmit the smoke of their furnaces through a subterraneous tunnel to the monumental-looking chimney on the picturesque knoll, shown in the drawing. By this means, a powerful furnace draught is obtained, corresponding to a height of fully three hundred feet.

As this mill spins warp yarn by throstles, weft yarn by mules, and weaves up both by power-looms, it exhibits in the collocation of its members an instructive specimen of the *philosophy of manufactures*. Both systems of spinning, namely, the continuous or by throstles, and the discontinuous or by mules, require the cotton to be prepared on the same system of machines; and therefore they must be both arranged subordinately to the *preparation rooms*. This arrangement has been considered in the true spirit of manufacturing economy by the engineer.

As the looms require the utmost stability, and an atmosphere rather humid than dry, they are placed on the ground-floor of the body of the building, as also in a shed behind it, to the number of about one thousand. The throstle-frames occupy the first and second stories of the main building; the mules, the fourth and fifth stories; each of these four apartments forming a noble gallery, three hundred feet long by fifty wide, and twelve feet high. The third story is the preparation gallery, intermediate between the throstles and mules, as it is destined to supply both with materials. Towards one end of this floor are distributed the carding-engines; towards the middle, the drawing-machines for arranging the cotton fibres in parallel lines, and forming them into uniform slivers, or soft narrow ribands; and towards the other end, the bobbin and fly-frames, or roving-machines, for converting the said slivers into slender porous cords, called rovings. These rovings are carried downstairs to be spun into warp-yarn on the throstles, and upstairs to be spun into weft (or sometimes warp) yarn on the mules.

The engine occupies an elevation of three stories at the right hand end of the mill. The stories immediately over it are devoted to the cleaning and lapping the cotton for the cards. Here are, 1. the willows for winnowing out the coarser impurities; 2. the blowing-machine for thoroughly opening out the cotton into clean individual fibres; and 3. the lapping-machine, for converting these fibres into a broad soft fleece like wadding, and coiling the fleece into cylindrical rolls. These laps are carried to the continuous carding-engines, and applied to their feed-aprons. The winding-machines, and a few mules, occupy the remaining apartments in the right wing. The attic story of the main building is appropriated to the machines for warping and dressing the yarn for the power-looms. The other wing of the mill is occupied with the counting-house, store-rooms, and apartments for winding the cotton on the large bobbins used for the warping-frame.

A staircase is placed in the corner of each wing, which has a horse-shoe shape, in order to furnish, in its interior, the tunnel space of the teagle or hoist apparatus, for raising and lowering the work-people and the goods from one floor to another. Andrew Ure. *The Philosophy of Manufactures*, 1835, 109–12

[Sir] Edwin Chadwick (1800–1890), the aggressive, ever-active disciple of Jeremy Bentham (1748–1842), played a notable part in producing the Reports of the Royal Commissions on factory labour (1833) and the Poor Laws (1834). From 1834 he was the energetic secretary to the Poor Law Commissioners and largely responsible for enforcing the hated new Act. He became increasingly interested in public health, and in 1842 published his famous 'Sanitary Report'; from 1848 to 1854 he was a commissioner on the Public Health Board. Here Chadwick describes the technical and social advantages of a new lay-out at the Deanston Mills.

49 On my return from Glasgow, I proceeded to visit and examine the cotton manufactory and machine-making works erected and carried on under the directions of Mr. James Smith, of Deanston, near Stirling, the inventor of the subsoil plough. . . .

The principle of the improvement of places of work, which constituted the chief object of attention at Deanston, was the erection of manufactories in one large flat or ground floor, instead of story piled upon story as in the old mode.

Mr. Smith had constructed a new department of the cotton-mill in one room or flat, which covered about half an acre of ground. The roof was composed of groined arches in divisional squares of 33 feet 6 inches, supported on cast-iron columns, which were hollow, and through which the drainage of the roof was effected. . . .

The height of this large room was 12 feet from the floor to the spring of the arches, and six feet rise, giving a height to the room in which the operatives were engaged of 18 feet. The height of the ordinary rooms in which the workpeople in manu-factories are engaged is not more than from 9 to 11 feet. This restricted space arises from various points of economy (now considered to be mistaken) in the old modes of constructing manufactories, which were first erected in towns where land was dear, and in times when the immediate economy of capital was of more pressing importance. The adverse consequences to the operatives are the restriction of space for air; that the heat and effluvia of the lower rooms are communicated to the rooms above; and that the difficulty of ventilating them is exceedingly great, especially in the wide rooms, where it is found to be practically extremely difficult to get a current of fresh air to pass through the centre. The like difficulties have been hereto-fore experienced in respect to the ventilation of large ships. There is also in the mills of the old construction the additional fatigue of ascending and descending to the higher rooms, and carrying material. To avoid this, in some instances, machinery is resorted to.

The ventilation through the side windows of large rooms is generally found to be imperfect and inconvenient in many of the processes, and annoying to the workpeople from the influx of the air in strong currents. The arrangements for ventilation through the roof of this room appeared to be highly advan-tageous. The light was brought in from above, through open-ings eight feet in diameter at the top of each groin, surmounted by domes or cones of glass, at the apex of which there were openings of about 16 inches in diameter, with covers that could be opened or shut at pleasure, to admit of ventilation. The better distribution of the light for the work from these openings was one advantage they appeared to possess over the ordinary mode of getting light from side windows.

The chief arrangements from below for ventilation were made by tunnels 10 feet distance from each other, carried across and underneath the floor of the building, and terminating in the open air on either side. The covers of these tunnels were perforated with holes of about an inch in diameter and 12 inches apart, disposed through the floor so as to occasion a wide and uniform distribution of fresh air throughout the whole building, on the same principle as that adopted for the admission of fresh air through the floor of the House of Commons. In winter time the fresh air admitted was warmed on the same principle, by pipes of hot water, to prevent the inconvenience of the admission of currents of cold air. The whole building was, from its size and arrangements, kept at a steady temperature, and appeared to be less susceptible than other buildings to atmospheric influence. The shaftings for the conveyance of the power were carried through the tunnels, and straps or belts from the shafts rise through the cover of the tunnels, and, by their motion, aid in promoting the circulation of the air. The possibility of fatal accidents from the persons being caught by the straps and wound round the shafts, was by this arrangement entirely prevented. The tunnelling under this arrangement constituted a boxing off of the whole of the shafting. Another advantage from the removal of the driving-straps from above was that the view over the whole room was entirely unimpeded.

Another structural improvement was in the use of a thin flooring of wood over the solid base of stone floors. The floor so arranged affords the solidity of the stone floor, and inconsiderable danger of combustion, whilst the advantages of the wooden surface to the workers were a diminution of swelled ankles and rheumatic affections of the joints, often produced by working bare-footed on stone floors.

There were no entries made from which I could obtain for comparison an account of the amount of sickness experienced by the workpeople in this new room, but it was obvious that the improvement must be considerable, and it was attested by the rosy and fresh countenances of the females and of the workpeople generally. A considerable improvement was manifest in the health of those workpeople who had previously worked in the older and less spacious rooms.

. . . The chief advantages of the improved arrangements of the places of work were, on the side of the workpeople, improved health; security for females and for the young against the dangers of fatal accidents, and less fatigue in the execution of the same amount of work. But beyond these the arrangement of the work in one room had moral advantages of high value. The bad manners and immoralities complained of as attendant on assemblages of workpeople of both sexes in manufactories, generally occur, as may be expected, in small rooms and places where few are employed, and that are secluded from superior inspection and from common observation. But whilst employed in this one large room, the young are under the inspection of the old; the children are in many instances under the inspection of parents, and all under the observation of the whole body of workers, and under the inspection of the employer. It was observed that the moral condition of the females in this room stood comparatively high. It would scarcely be practicable to discriminate the moral effects arising from one cause where several are in operation; but it was stated by ministers that there were fewer cases of illegitimacy and less vice observable among the population engaged in this manufactory than amongst the surrounding population of the labouring class. The comparative circumstances of that population were such as, when examined, would establish the conclusion that it must be so.

The first expense of such a building is higher than a manufactory of the old construction; but it appeared to possess countervailing economical advantages to the capitalist, the chief of which are,—this same facility of constant general supervision, the increase of the certainty of superintendence, and the reduction of the numbers of subordinate managers, the increase of efficiency of management, and a diminution of its expense. Another advantage arose to the manufacturer in the superior action of the machinery. In mills of the ordinary construction the machinery is frequently deranged in its structure, and put out of order by the yielding and unsteadiness of the upper floors. The machinery erected on the ground floor has a firm basis, and a steady and more durable action. The other advantages presented were, the saving of labour in transporting the material from one process to another, a labour which is often considerable in expense, as well as in inconvenience, in lifting it into the higher rooms; the reduction of the hazard of fire, and consequently in expense of insurance against it, as fire could scarcely take place, and certainly could not rapidly extend in a manufactory so constructed. These several sources of economy Mr. Smith calculated would more than compensate for any increase of ground-rent, even if the building were erected on land costing 1,000 *l.* per acre. Mr. Marshall, of Leeds, on consulting with Mr. Smith, has constructed a new manufactory (on the principle of that in Deanston) in Leeds, where ground is valuable. This manufactory covers more than two acres of ground, and is reported to be eminently successful. Power looms are frequently arranged in buildings of one story, and I was informed of another manufactory in Lancashire, nearly as large as that of Messrs. Marshalls, built on one floor, but it did not appear to possess the arrangements for ventilation and warming, and the other arrangements necessary to the complete action of a place of work on the plan of that at Deanston. Edwin Chadwick. *Report on the Sanitary Condition of the Labouring Population and on the Means of its Improvement,* 1842, 240–4

During 1868 David Bremner, an Edinburgh writer, contributed a series of papers to *The Scotsman* newspaper on the state of Scottish industry. An amended version was published, as a remarkable book, in 1869. Bremner clearly shared other mid-

Victorians' sense of pride in their achievement, but he hoped that his volume would be used in the 'lively discussion on technical education'. The extract below describes a major Glasgow enterprise after the difficulties of the 'cotton famine' during the American Civil War.

---

50 Among the most extensive cotton factories in Scotland are those of Messrs. A. & A. Galbraith, situated at Oakbank and St. Rollox, Glasgow. The factories comprise two immense ranges of somewhat irregular buildings. The original portions were erected many years ago, and the successive additions may be traced in the different tints of the masonry. The joint establishments cannot be pointed to as models, so far as the buildings are concerned; but they are filled with machinery of the finest and most recent construction, and their internal economy is equal to that of any other mills in the country. In the spinning department there are 95,000 mule and throstle spindles, the produce of which is made into cloth by 1532 power-looms. There are several large steam-engines, the aggregate indicated force of which is 1600 horse power. 1700 persons, of whom only 100 are males, are employed; and the quantity of cloth made is 350,000 yards a-week, or 17,000,000 yards a-year. All the cloth is of the plain kind for printing and dyeing.

. . . As the cotton is subjected to one operation after another, it is elevated from floor to floor, according to the arrangements of the successive machines; so that by the time the spinning processes are completed, the cotton has been elevated to the fifth or sixth floor. Most of the machines are attended by women or girls, whose work is exceedingly light, and much more healthy than it used to be.

It would be impossible to conceive machines more perfectly adapted to their purpose than those which crowd the spacious floors of Messrs. Galbraith's factories. Each seems to work with a will and instinct of its own, and no one can witness their operations without admiring the ingenuity that devised their thousands of parts and brought them all into harmonious play. Fingers of iron and wood work more deftly, and with apparently more delicacy of touch, than fingers of flesh and blood could ever do; and the finest productions of the Indian hand-spinners are surpassed by the gossamer-like threads which the self-acting spinning-mule produces by hundreds at a time.   David Bremner. *The Industries of Scotland. Their Rise, Progress, and Present Condition*, Edinburgh, 1869, 291, 293

Notes

PART ONE: BEFORE THE FACTORY SYSTEM

The Norwich Worsted Industry On the decline of Norwich see Sir J. H. Clapham. 'The Transference of the Worsted Industry from Norfolk to the West Riding', *Economic Journal*, xx, 1910; Miss M. F. Lloyd Pritchard. 'The Decline of Norwich', *Economic History Review*, 2s, iii, 1951; J. K. Edwards. 'The Decline of the Norwich Textile Industry', *Yorkshire Bulletin of Economic and Social Research*, xvi, 1964. Eden's book has been reprinted (1966).

The Yorkshire Woollen Industry Yorkshire's development has been described by several modern authors, notably Herbert Heaton. *The Yorkshire Woollen and Worsted Industries from the Earliest Times up to the Industrial Revolution*, Oxford, 1920, 1965; E. Lipson. *History of the Woollen and Worsted Industries*, 1921, 1968, *A History of Wool and Wool Manufacture*, 1953; W. B. Crump, *The Leeds Woollen Industry, 1780–1820*, Leeds, 1931; W. B. Crump and Gertrude Ghorbal. *History of the Huddersfield Woollen Industry*, Huddersfield, 1935; E. M. Sigsworth. *Black Dyke Mills. A History*, Liverpool, 1958. On Defoe see J. R. Moore. *Daniel Defoe, Citizen of the Modern World*, Chicago, 1958; J. H. Andrews. 'Defoe and the Sources of his Tour', *Geographical Journal*, cxxxvi, 1960; F. Bastian, 'Defoe's Tour and the Historian', *History Today*, xvii, 1967. Defoe's *Tour* has been republished, ed G. D. H. Cole, 1927, 1968; see also G. D. H. Cole. *Persons and Periods*, 1938, 1945, 1969, ch 1–2. A new impression of James' work has been issued (1968) and Aikin's book has been republished (Newton Abbot, 1968).

The Southern Woollen Industries The western woollen areas are examined by D. M. Hunter. *The West of England Woollen Industry* 1910; G. D. Ramsay. *The Wiltshire Woollen Industry in the Sixteenth and Seventeenth Centuries*, 1943, 1965; R. P. Beckinsale (ed). *The Trowbridge Woollen Industry . . . 1804–1824*, Devizes, 1951; K. G. Ponting. *A History of the West of England Cloth Industry*, 1957; E. A. L. Moir. 'The Gentlemen Clothiers: a Study of the Organisation of the Gloucestershire Cloth Industry, 1750–1835', in H. P. R. Finberg (ed). *Gloucestershire Studies*, Leicester, 1957; J. de L. Mann. 'Clothiers and Weavers in Wiltshire during the Eighteenth Century', in L. S. Pressnell (ed). *Studies in the Industrial Revolution*, 1960, *Documents illustrating the Wiltshire Textile Trades in the Eighteenth Century*, Devizes, 1964. On East Anglia see also K. H. Burley. 'An Essex Clothier of the Eighteenth Century', *Econ Hist Rev*, 2s, xi, 1958.

A Mercantile Community See W. E. Minchinton. 'The Merchants in England in the Eighteenth Century', in B. E. Supple (ed). *The Entrepreneur*, Harvard, 1957. Several biographies are given in Fox Bourne's book (here quoted) and R. V. Taylor. *Biographia Leodiensis*, Leeds, 1865; see also R. G. Wilson. 'The Fortunes of a Leeds Merchant House, 1780–1820', *Business History*, ix, 1967, 'Records for the Study of the Leeds Woollen Manufacturers, 1700–1830', *Archives*, viii, 1967.

The Lancashire Cotton Industry On the cotton industry's early history see also G. W. Daniels. *The Early English Cotton Industry*, Manchester, 1920; A. P. Wadsworth and J. de L. Mann. *The Cotton Trade and Industrial Lancashire, 1600–1780*, Manchester, 1931. Baines' volume has been republished (intro W. H. Chaloner, 1968).

The Hosiery Industry A celebrated but not entirely reliable account is Gravenor Henson. *The Civil, Political and Mechanical History of the Framework-Knitters*, Nottingham, 1831. Modern views are given in J. D. Chambers. 'The Worshipful Company of Framework Knitters', *Economica*, ix, 1929; *Nottinghamshire in the Eighteenth Century*, 1932, 1966; E. G. Nelson. 'The Putting-Out System in the English Framework-Knitting Industry', *Journal of Economic and Business History*, ii, 1930; F. A. Wells. *The British Hosiery Trade: Its History and Organisation*, 1935; Stanley Pigott. *Hollins. A Study of Industry, 1784–1949*, Nottingham, 1949; R. S. Fitton and A. P. Wadsworth. *The Strutts and the Arkwrights, 1758–1830*, Manchester, 1958; C. L. Hacker. 'William Strutt of Derby (1756–1830)', *Journal of the Derbyshire Archaeological and Natural History Society*, lxxx, 1959.

The Silk Industry   See G. B. Hertz. 'The English Silk Industry in the Eighteenth Century', *English Historical Review*, xxiv, 1909; W. H. Chaloner. 'Sir Thomas Lombe (1685–1739) and the British Silk Industry', *History Today*, iii, 1953, reprinted in W. H. Chaloner. *People and Industries*, 1963. On the ribbon-weaving industry see John Prest. *The Industrial Revolution in Coventry*, Oxford, 1960; Miss V. W. Challoner (ed). *Master and Artisan in Victorian England*, 1969.

The Linen Industry   On subsequent developments see W. G. Rimmer. 'The Flax Industry', *Leeds Journal*, 1954, 'Castle Foregate Flax Mill, Shrewsbury', *Transactions of the Shropshire Archaeological Society*, 1957–8, *Marshalls of Leeds, Flax Spinners, 1788–1886*, Cambridge, 1960; D. Chapman. 'William Brown of Dundee, 1791–1864: Management in a Scottish Flax Mill', *Explorations in Entrepreneurial History*, iv, 1953. See also Conrad Gill. *The Rise of the Irish Linen Industry*, Oxford, 1925, 1964; A. K. Longfield. 'History of the Irish Linen and Cotton Printing Industry in the Eighteenth Century', *Journal of the Royal Society of Antiquaries in England*, 7s, vii, 1937. Warden's book was reprinted in 1967.

The Weaver   The first accurate translation of Engels' work, with critical notes, is the edition prepared by W. O. Henderson and W. H. Chaloner (Oxford, 1958). For varied views see Gustav Meyer. *Friedrich Engels*, 1934; Mick Jenkins, *Frederick Engels in Manchester*, Manchester, 1951; W. O. Henderson and W. H. Chaloner. 'Engels and the England of the 1840s', *History Today*, vi, 1956, 'Friedrich Engels in Manchester', *Memoirs and Proceedings of the Manchester Literary and Philosophical Society*, xcviii, 1957; Grace Carlton. *Friedrich Engels. The Shadow Prophet*,

1965. On the weavers see Duncan Bythell. 'The Handloom Weavers in the English Cotton Industry during the Industrial Revolution: Some Problems', *Econ Hist Rev*, 2s, xvii, 1964, *The Handloom Weavers*, Cambridge, 1969; E. M. Sigsworth. 'The End of Handloom Weaving', *Bradford Textile Society Journal*, 1957–8; J. T. Ward, 'The Literary Weavers', ibid, 1968–9. Bamford's book has been republished (intro W. H. Chaloner, 1967).

PART TWO: THE ENTREPRENEURS AND INVENTORS

The Climate of Opinion   See Jacob Viner. *Adam Smith, 1776–1826*, Chicago, 1928; John Rae. *Life of Adam Smith*, 1898, intro J. Viner, 1965; W. R. Scott. *Adam Smith as Student and Professor*, 1937, 1968; Lord Robbins. *The Theory of Economic Policy in English Classical Political Economy*, 1952; Aileen Smiles. *Samuel Smiles and his Surroundings*, 1956. Smith's book has regularly been reprinted (for instance, intro E. R. A. Seligman, 1931) and Smiles' work has also been republished (intro Asa Briggs, 1958). See also R. E. Scholfield. *The Lunar Society of Birmingham*, Oxford, 1963.

The Spinning Inventions   On the development of cotton see J. A. Mann. *The Cotton Trade of Great Britain*, 1860, 1968; Thomas Ellison. *The Cotton Trade of Great Britain*, 1886, 1968; S. J. Chapman. *The Lancashire Cotton Industry*, Manchester, 1904; J. L. and Barbara Hammond. *The Skilled Labourer*, 1919, *The Rise of Modern Industry*, 1926; G. Unwin, A. Hulme and G. Taylor. *Samuel Oldknow and the Arkwrights*, Manchester, 1924; H. C. Cameron. *Samuel Crompton*, 1951; S. Aspin and S. D. Chapman. *James Hargreaves and the Spinning Jenny*, 1964; S. D. Chapman. *The Early Factory Masters*, Newton Abbot, 1967. See also W. H. Marwick. 'The Cotton Industry and the Industrial Revolution in Scotland', *Scottish Historical Review*. xxi, 1924; G. M. Mitchell. 'The English and Scottish Cotton Industries: A Study in Inter-relations', ibid, xxii, 1925; Frances Collier. 'An Early Factory Community', *Economic History*, ii, 1930;

J. J. Monaghan. 'The Rise and Fall of the Belfast Cotton Industry', *Irish Historical Studies*, iii, 1943; J. D. Marshall. 'The Cotton Mills of the Upper Lean', *Transactions of the Thoroton Society*, lx, 1956; R. Thornhill. 'The Arkwright Cotton Mill at Bakewell', *J. Derbyshire Arch & Nat Hist Soc*, lxxix, 1959; M. H. Mackenzie. 'The Bakewell Mill and the Arkwrights', ibid, lxxix, 1959; J. Lindsay. 'An Early Industrial Community. The Evans' Cotton Mill at Darley Abbey, Derbyshire, 1783–1810', *Business History Review*, xxxiv, 1960; W. H. Chaloner. 'The Stockdale Family, the Wilkinson Brothers and the Cotton Mills at Cark-in-Cartmel, c 1782–1800', *Transactions of the Cumberland and Westmorland Antiquarian and Archaeological Society*, ns, lxiv, 1964; S. D. Chapman. 'The Transition to the Factory System in the Midlands Cotton-Spinning Industry', *Econ Hist Rev*, 2s, xviii, 1965.

The Power-Loom For a sociological view see N. J. Smelser. *Social Change in the Industrial Revolution*, 1959. On the Industrial Revolution generally see L. C. A. Knowles. *The Industrial and Commercial Revolutions*, 1922; P. Mantoux. *The Industrial Revolution in the Eighteenth Century*, 1928; T. S. Ashton. *The Industrial Revolution, 1760–1830*, Oxford, 1948, *An Economic History of England. The Eighteenth Century*, 1955; W. H. B. Court. *A Concise Economic History of Britain from 1750 to Recent Times*, Cambridge, 1954; Phyllis Deane. *The First Industrial Revolution*, Cambridge, 1965; M. W. Flinn. *Origins of the Industrial Revolution*, 1966; Peter Mathias. *The First Industrial Nation*, 1969. Guest's book has been reprinted (1968).

Steam-Power See J. Lord. *Capital and Steam Power, 1750–1800*, 1923, 1968; H. W. Dickinson and R. Jenkins. *James Watt and the Steam Engine*, 1927; H. W. Dickinson. *A Short History of the Steam Engine*, Cambridge, 1939, intro A. E. Musson, 1968; A. E. Musson and E. Robinson. 'The Early Growth of Steam Power', *Econ Hist Rev*, 2s, xi, 1959, 'Science and Industry in the late Eighteenth Century', ibid, 2s, xiii, 1960, 'The Origins of Engineering in Lancashire', *Journal of Economic History*, xx, 1960; L. T. C. Rolt. *Thomas Newcomen*, Dawlish, 1963, *James*

N

Watt, 1962. Cf A. P. Usher. *A History of Mechanical Inventions*, Harvard, 1954 edn; Sir Eric Roll. *An Early Experiment in Industrial Organisation*, 1930, 1968.

The Organisers On the Peels see Norman Gash. *Mr Secretary Peel*, 1961; on Oldknow Unwin et al, op cit; on Sinclair, Rosalind Mitchison. *Agricultural Sir John*, 1962; on Catrine, James Paterson. *History of the County of Ayr*, Ayr, Edinburgh, 1847, J. T. Ward. 'Ayrshire Landed Estates in the Nineteenth Century', *Ayrshire Collections*, 2s, viii, 1969; on Owen, R. D. Owen. *Threading My Way*, 1874, Frank Podmore. *Robert Owen*, 1906, G. D. H. Cole. *Life of Robert Owen*, 1925, 1930, intro Margaret Cole, 1968, Margaret Cole. *Robert Owen of New Lanark*, 1953, W. H. Chaloner. 'Robert Owen, Peter Drinkwater and the Early Factory System in Manchester', *Bulletin of the John Rylands Library*, xxxvii, 1954, and Owen's *Life*, 2 vols, 1857, 1968; on Heathcoat, W. Gore Allen. *John Heathcoat and his Heritage*, 1958, D. E. Varley, *John Heathcoat, 1783–1861*, Newton Abbot, 1969; on Gott, Herbert Heaton. 'Benjamin Gott and the Anglo-American Cloth Trade', *J Econ & Bus Hist*, ii, 1929, 'Benjamin Gott and the Industrial Revolution in Yorkshire', *Econ Hist Rev*, iii, 1931; on Manners' visit to the Grants, Charles Whibley. *Lord John Manners and his Friends*, 1925, i, and on the background J. T. Ward. 'Young England', *History Today*, xvi, 1966. See also Charles Wilson. 'The Entrepreneur in the Industrial Revolution', *History*, xlii, 1957.

The Employers Owen's *New View* was reprinted (intro G. D. H. Cole, 1927) and in vol. i A of Owen's *Life*, 1857, 1968. See P. Gorb. 'Robert Owen as a Businessman', *Bulletin of the Business History Society*, xxv, 1951; J. F. C. Harrison. *Robert Owen and the Owenites in Britain and America*, 1969; and on Wood, J. T. Ward. 'Two Pioneers in Industrial Reform', *Bradford Textile Society Journal*, 1962–3.

PART THREE: THE FACTORY SYSTEM ESTABLISHED

The Factory System For a modern assessment of the new problems of the factory system see Sidney Pollard. 'Investment, Consumption and the Industrial Revolution', *Econ Hist Rev*, 2s, xi, 1958, 'Factory Discipline in the Industrial Revolution', ibid, xvi, 1963, 'Capital Accounting in the Industrial Revolution', *Yorks Bull*, xv, 1963. 'The Factory Village in the Industrial Revolution', *English Historical Review*, lxxix, 1964. 'Fixed Capital in the Industrial Revolution in Britain', *Journal of Economic History*, xxiv, 1964, *The Genesis of Modern Management*, 1965, 1969. Ure's book has been reprinted (1967).

The Lancashire Cotton Industry On the expansion of cotton see also A. Redford. *Manchester Merchants and Foreign Trade, 1794–1858*, Manchester, 1934; A. J. Taylor. 'Concentration and Specialization in the Lancashire Cotton Industry', *Econ Hist Rev*, 2s, i, 1949; Mark Blaug. 'Productivity of Capital in the Lancashire Cotton Industry during the Nineteenth Century', ibid, xiii, 1961; R. Smith. 'Manchester as a Centre for the Manufacture and Merchanting of Cotton Goods', *University of Birmingham Historical Journal*, iv, 1953; Frances Collier (ed R. S. Fitton). *The Family Economy of the Working Classes in the Cotton Industry, 1784–1833*, Manchester, 1964; B. W. Clapp. *John Owens*, Manchester, 1966. For an important reassessment of 'Peterloo' see Robert Walmsley, *Peterloo: The Case Re-opened*, Manchester, 1969.

The Woollen and Worsted Industries Aspects of the woollen and worsted industries' development are examined in Edward Collinson. *History of the Worsted Trade*, Bradford, 1851; H. D. Fong. *The Triumph of the Factory System in England*, Tientsin, 1930. Head's book has been republished (intro W. H. Chaloner, 1968). On the identification of the authors of the *Morning Chronicle* reports see E. P. Thompson. 'The Political Education of Henry Mayhew', *Victorian Studies*, xi, 1967. On aspects of the Yorkshire blanket trade see F. J. Glover. 'The

Rise of the Heavy Woollen Trade of the West Riding of Yorkshire in the Nineteenth Century', *Business History*, iv, 1961, 'Thomas Cook and the American Blanket Trade in the Nineteenth Century', *Business History Review*, xxxv, 1961.

Change in the West   On Cobbett see E. I. Carlyle. *William Cobbett*, 1904; Lewis Melville. *The Life and Letters of William Cobbett*, 1913; G. D. H. Cole. *The Life of William Cobbett*, 1947 edn. *Rural Rides* has been reprinted (ed G. D. H. and Margaret Cole, 1930; intro Asa Briggs, 1957). On Bischoff see R. V. Taylor, op cit, 409–11; Bischoff's book has been reprinted (1968).

The New Factories   See also Ure. *Cotton Manufacture*, i, 297–305. On Chadwick see S. E. Finer. *The Life and Times of Sir Edwin Chadwick*, 1952; R. A. Lewis, *Edwin Chadwick and the Public Health Movement*, 1952; M. W. Flinn, introduction to reissue of the 'Sanitary Report', Edinburgh, 1965. On Scottish industry see Henry Hamilton. *The Industrial Revolution in Scotland*, Oxford, 1932, *An Economic History of Scotland in the Eighteenth Century*, Oxford, 1963; John Butt. *The Industrial Archaeology of Scotland*, Newton Abbot, 1967. Bremner's book has been reprinted (intro J. Butt and I. L. Donnachie, Newton Abbot, 1969).

Acknowledgments

At various times, many people have given me generous aid in the work which has led to this book. In particular, I am grateful to the late Mr F. R. Salter, OBE, of Magdalene College, Cambridge, for his kindly and patient guidance and encouragement. Other friends have given or lent me books or transcriptions: Mr Frank Beckwith of Leeds, the late Colonel G. W. Ferrand, OBE, of Oving, Mr G. F. Foster of Ashton-under-Lyne, Canon J. C. Gill of Worthing, the late Mr G. G. Hopkinson of Brighouse, Mr Derick Mirfin of London, Mr J. Lupton of Guiseley, Miss L. R. Walker, Mr H. Bilton and Mr J. H. Macdonald of Bradford, and my colleagues Dr J. Butt, Dr J. H. Treble, Mr J. R. Hume and Dr W. H. Fraser of the University of Strathclyde have been especially helpful. I am greatly indebted to Mr Douglas Keighley of the Thoresby Society for kindly permitting me to republish material from W. B. Crump's volume on *The Leeds Woollen Industry*.

Many librarians have helped my work, often at considerable inconvenience to themselves. I must acknowledge my indebtedness to the librarians and staffs at Aberdeen, Ashton-under-Lyne, Ayr, Bingley, Birmingham, Bolton, Bradford, Bury, Cambridge University, Derby, Dewsbury, Dundee, Dundee University, Edinburgh, Glasgow, Glasgow University, Halifax, Huddersfield, Keighley, Kilmarnock, Leeds, Leeds City, London University, Manchester, Oldham, Paisley, Preston, Rochdale, Scottish National, Stockport and Todmorden libraries.

I am grateful to Miss A. M. McEleney for typing an often difficult script. And I am also obliged for my family's tolerance during the preparation of the book. For the contents I am solely responsible.

Index